THE CHR[...]

ISSUES
and
answers

~ ❧ ❧ ~

GARY MAEDER WITH DON WILLIAMS

A Division of G/L Publications
Glendale, California, U.S.A.

Other good Regal reading on related subjects:
Dr. James Dobson Talks about God's Will, James Dobson
Dr. James Dobson Talks about Love, James Dobson
Heavy Questions, Dave Grant
Jesus Person Maturity Manual, David Wilkerson
Lord, Make My Life Count, Raymond C. Ortlund
Miracles Happen in Group Bible Study, Albert J. Wollen
Now That I'm a Christian, Vols. 1 & 2, Chuck Miller
Praying: How to Start and Keep Going, Bobb Biehl/James W. Hagelganz
Spiritual Renewal, James Kennedy
The Gift Within You, Ray C. Stedman
The Other Side of Morality, Fritz Ridenour
This Is the Life, James Kennedy

Except where otherwise indicated, the Scriptures quoted
are from the *New American Standard Bible*.
© The Lockman Foundation, 1971. Used by permission.

Published by
Regal Books Division, G/L Publications
Glendale, California 91209, U.S.A.

Library of Congress Catalog Card No. (76-29258)
ISBN 0-8307-0470-1

Revised Edition, 1976
First Published as *God's Will for Your Life*

CONTENTS

PREFACE

The Christian Life: Issues and Answers: was born out of the need for following up new Christians reached through the Deputation Program of the First Presbyterian Church of Hollywood. During his senior year at the University of California at Los Angeles, Gary Maeder wrote several of the outlines contained in this series for a Bible study group he was leading in Redondo Beach. Under the guidance of Don Williams, who reviewed the outlines and suggested changes and additions where appropriate, and with the assistance of Terri Williams Dawson, Gary wrote the remaining outlines during the following year.

These outlines are designed to deal in an introductory fashion with some of the basic spiritual, moral, social and intellectual aspects of our life with Christ. We have prayerfully sought to base all our ideas upon the Bible, which we strongly affirm to be God's inspired Word to us. We have accordingly provided references from Scripture to support our comments whenever possible. However, in most cases, to conserve space we have not quoted the verses themselves. We cannot over emphasize the importance of your looking up these references as you read, and in all other ways possible subjecting these outlines, as you would anything else, to the ultimate test of conformity to God's Word.

It is our prayer that these outlines will aid you not only in *your* walk with the Lord Jesus Christ but also in your striving to present *others* complete in Him. A number of Christians in various states across the country have found them useful for group studies, especially for Christians who are relatively new to the study of God's Word and who want to learn where to look in the Bible for answers to basic questions that pop up frequently.

Many of the ideas we have incorporated into these outlines are not original, and much of our effort has been devoted to drawing material out of various sources, organizing it into outline form and adding scriptural references to support the text wherever possible. We have accordingly attempted to give appropriate credit in the bibliographies at the end of most of the outlines, and occasionally in the body of the outline as well, to these gifted men of God to whom we all owe many insights.

We are especially indebted to Terri Williams Dawson for her assistance on four of the outlines.

Gary Maeder
Don Williams

*"Therefore also we have as our ambition
. . . to be pleasing to Him."*

—*II Corinthians 5:9*

PART ONE

GROWING UP INTO CHRIST

1

DISCOVERING
GOD'S WILL
FOR *YOUR* LIFE

I. BASIC PRINCIPLES

A. God has a purpose for your life, and you are individually loved and called into His family by Him. Luke 15:3-7; I Peter 5:6, 7. There are three general categories of reasons why we should seek to determine and carry out God's will for our lives.

1. Obligation to God—God created man in His own image to have fellowship with Him. In spite of the fact that every one of us has snubbed God in rebelling against His authority over our lives, He considers us worth saving. In His mercy, God took the initiative by becoming man in Jesus of Nazareth to live a perfect life, to lay down His life voluntarily on the cross to pay the penalty for our rebellion against His Father, and to rise again from the grave to prove that His claims to be God were true and to conquer death so that we might spend eternity with Him. In response to this unparalleled love shown to us by God, we, like Jesus, should consider our "food" to be doing the will of God. John 4:34; Matthew 7:21; Philippians 2:13; I John 4:9, 10.

2. Obligation to self—Christianity is not just "pie in the sky, by and by," but abundant, eternal life which begins *now* even though complete fulfillment will come only upon Christ's return in glory. John 10:10; I Corinthians 2:9; Revelation 21:4. As your Creator, Redeemer, and Sanctifier, God knows better than you—or anyone else—what is best for you. God's will for your life is precisely that which is best for *you*. Consequently, it is imperative for your sake that you continually seek to determine God's "good, acceptable, and perfect" will for your life and to act in accordance with that determination. Romans 12:1, 2.

3. Obligation to others—The mark of our discipleship is love for others, and God wants to bring others into His family *through us*, that we all might grow into maturity in Christ. John 13:34, 35; I John 4:11. The body of believers in Jesus Christ is to be a lighthouse of hope and love in the midst of the darkness of despair and hate in our lost world. Philippians 2:15. We are to serve Jesus by serving others, particularly disadvantaged others. Matthew 25:31-40; James 1:27. The Church of Jesus Christ is to *be* Jesus Christ to the world.

B. The will of God is frequently approached from the "program" angle: What college, if any, does God want me to attend? What occupation does He want me to enter? Who is His choice for my life partner? These are all valid questions, but God's will for you is not fundamentally a college, vocation, or spouse, but is rather a personal, growing *relationship* with Him. In short, it's not what you do; it's what you are. This suggests a crucial distinction.

1. The will of God concerning the formation of our *characters* is universal: we are all to be conformed to Jesus Christ and be led by, and display the fruit (love, joy, peace, patience, kindness, goodness, faithfulness, gentleness, and self-control—Galatians 5:22, 23) of the Holy Spirit. Romans 8:29; Philippians 3:20, 21.

2. The will of God concerning our *service* is individual: since we haven't all been given the same spiritual gifts and talents, the ways in which you are to serve God depend upon the particular set of gifts and talents with which you have been entrusted. Romans 12:3-8; I Corinthians 12-14; Ephesians 4:7-16; I Peter 4:10, 11.

C. The overwhelming majority of God's will for your life concerns your character and is revealed in the Bible. Consequently, nothing in your day should be allowed to crowd out your time spent alone with the Lord reading His Word and in prayer. II Timothy 3:16, 17. Two particularly revealing passages on the will of God are Romans 12-15 and I Thessalonians 4-5.

D. Discovering the will of God for your life is thus primarily a matter of acceptance and not of guidance: "If any man is willing to do His will, he shall know of the teaching, whether it is of God, or whether I speak from Myself." John 7:17. However, in the remainder of this outline, we shall consider only how to discover that portion of God's will for our lives that concerns our particular service to Him and accordingly is not directly spelled out in the Bible.

E. The basic principle of guidance is that God does not unfold before us the entire blueprint of His purpose for the rest of our lives, but that He does promise to give each of us sufficient light to take the next step. Proverbs 2:3-6; 3:5, 6; Matthew 7:7; James 1:5.

II. PREREQUISITES FOR A FULLER KNOWLEDGE OF GOD'S WILL FOR YOUR LIFE

A. You must be a child of God, i.e. you must know Jesus Christ as your personal Lord and Savior. Jesus wants to fellowship with each of us but can do so only if we are willing to give ourselves unconditionally to Him. John 6:29; Revelation 3:20.

B. You must confess to the Lord any sin in your life of which you are aware. Sin, which is characterized by active rebellion and/or passive indifference toward God, can never hurt our *relationship* with God—we are His children. John 1:12; 8:27-29; Romans 8:38, 39. But sin does block our *fellowship* with Him until we have repented (turned away from) and asked God's forgiveness for our sin. Romans 6:23; I John 1:8-10.

C. You must obey Him in every area of your life where He has already been specific with you. "Light obeyed increases light; light rejected brings night." God wants to reveal more of His plan to us but generally chooses not to reveal more than we are able to digest, so *we* are the ones to blame for our not knowing more of His will for our lives. John 8:12. In fact, even the light we have received may be taken away from us if we persist in disobeying it. Matthew 13:11,12.

D. You must be willing to obey whatever command He may choose to give you in the future. John 7:17. Much too often our actions indicate that, whatever we may say, we think we know better than God what is best for us. The condition of an enlightened mind is a totally surrendered heart. Our arrogance seems often to stem from our fear of what God's will for our lives *might* be, and we need to realize the irrationality of such fear. Matthew 7:11; Romans 8:32. God is not the "Cosmic Killjoy" who wants us to be miserable! We need to seek to begin to grasp the divine perspective, which, for example, sees testing as an instrument used by God to conform us to the image of Christ. Romans 5: 3-5; James 1:2-4.

III. HOW GOD WILL GUIDE YOU

A. By your reading the Bible daily with an open heart and mind, *expecting* God to give you concrete directives as you diligently search for the commands and the underlying principles in His Word—Psalm 119:105.

B. By the inward witness of the Holy Spirit, who is God's gift to all believers at the time of their dedication of their lives to Christ—The Holy Spirit will often convict you through

11

prayer and allow you to have no peace until you have carried out some particular aspect of His will for your life. Read the short book of Jonah in the Old Testament and the account of Philip and the Ethiopian eunuch in Acts 8:26-40 as excellent examples of this type of conviction and leading.

C. By a prayerful assessment of your circumstances—For example, in choosing a college to attend, a student seeking the Lord's will may want to read the catalogues from several colleges, talk to people who have attended them, and consider carefully which school can best help him to achieve his objectives. God will also open and close doors for us to guide us: a person who applies for a job and is rejected can be sure that God's will for him, at least at this time, is to be found elsewhere. Many of us tend to over-rely on external circumstances and to forget to attempt to view them from God's perspective. Acts 16:6-10.

D. By the counsel of other Christians who are committed to doing God's will—This is most often neglected in general, but as Christ's body on earth we are all to be on the lookout for ways in which we can serve other members of the body of believers and also to be seeking the advice of others on difficult matters. "Where there is no guidance, the people fall, but in abundance of counselors there is victory." Proverbs 11:14. However, we must never evade the responsibility of deciding *as individuals* what God wants us to do. For example, Paul continued on to Jerusalem in spite of the protestations of Christians in Tyre and Caesarea. Acts 19:21; 20:22; 21:4; 10-14.

IV. MISTAKES TO AVOID

A. Don't become legalistic.

  1. Some decisions follow automatically from others: once I had concluded that God wanted me at UCLA, I didn't need to pray about whether or not to send my application for admission in.

  2. The Christian not only does what God tells him to do but

12

also *anticipates* what God wants him to do and does it almost without being told.

3. There are certain areas of your life in which God has left you free to consult your own "sanctified common sense," e.g. the question of what shirt or dress to wear today.

B. Don't regard God's will as something you are to *do* at certain times (e.g. by going to church Sunday morning or to Bible study Tuesday evening) but as something you are to *be in* at all times. The will of God is a relationship—not a program. Our lives are to be integrated throughout—not segmented. For example, I believe that even something as mundane as brushing my teeth after a meal is part of God's will for my life.

C. Don't fall into the trap of thinking that God's will is so bizarre that we cannot or should not use our own reason, illumined by the Holy Spirit, in seeking to discover it. Guidance does not come to an empty mind, but to a heart full of the love of Jesus Christ. Therefore, as good stewards of the manifold grace of God, let's make full use of our reasoning capacities in making decisions. God gave us minds for a reason, and Paul says that Christians "have the mind of Christ." I Corinthians 2:16.

D. Don't get hung up on looking for subjective confirmation for every decision you make. Pray for guidance, be alert to God's leading, make decisions as necessary, and accept on faith (unless and until He indicates otherwise) that your decisions were the right ones.

E. In going to the Bible for guidance on specific matters, don't take verses out of their context by using the "close-the-eyes, open-the-Bible, point-the-finger, and read-the-verse" approach. If you do not know where in the Bible to look for the answer to a specific problem or question, seek the advice of some Christian you know who at this point has a better grasp of the Bible than you. Moreover, prepare yourself for times like these by beginning, if you haven't done so already, your own daily study of God's Word.

F. Don't be overly suspicious of your own desires. Of course, they will not always accord with God's will, but as you become more and more conformed to Jesus Christ, your attitudes and desires will become the ones He wants you to have. Psalm 37:4.

G. Don't think that your being in God's will exempts you from all problems and stress. Neither Job nor Paul, to name but two strong men of God, had a trouble-free life. However, you should try to determine the cause(s) of your problems, since failure to trust and obey God is definitely the source of many of our problems.

H. Don't take disobedience to God lightly, for by disobeying Him we remove ourselves from fellowship with Him, but at the same time don't forget that through Christ's death for us on the cross, forgiveness and the return to fellowship with God are ours if we repent and ask forgiveness for our sin. Peter openly denied our Lord three times (John 18:15-27) but was forgiven and returned to fellowship with the risen Jesus (John 21:15-23). See also I John 1:8-10.

I. Even if it seems that no alternative open to you can possibly be God's will for you, don't despair. Instead, do what the Psalmist frequently speaks of—*wait* upon God. "Make me know Thy ways, O Lord . . . for Thee I wait all the day." Psalm 25:4, 5. His promise to us is unfading: "I will instruct you and teach you in the way which you should go; I will counsel you with My eye upon you." Psalm 32:8. See also Jeremiah 42:7.

J. Don't become discouraged if you feel that you aren't growing spiritually as fast as you'd like, but be strengthened by the Word of God daily and allow Him to work within and through you as He pleases. It is *our* responsibility to present our bodies to God for His use, but it is *His* responsibility (and promise) to transform us. Romans 12:1, 2. "And I am sure that God who began the good work within you will keep right on helping you grow in his grace until his task within you is finally finished on that day when Jesus Christ returns." Philippians 1:6 (Living Bible).

K. Finally, as the late Dr. Henrietta Mears used to say, you can't steer a parked car, so get moving!

V. BIBLIOGRAPHY

Little, Paul. "God's Will for Me and World Evangelism," *Christ the Liberator.* Inter-Varsity Press, 1971.

2

ALONE
WITH GOD

I. WHY WE SHOULD SPEND
TIME ALONE WITH GOD

A. God desires our fellowship. He created us so that He might enjoy a relationship with us. John 4:23; Revelation 3:20.

B. We desire His fellowship, for He is our heavenly Father, the source of every good gift. James 1:17. Accordingly, we seek His fellowship, sometimes with others and sometimes alone.

C. Taking time out to be alone with God reminds us of His *continual* presence in our lives. Psalm 16:7-11. He has promised never to desert or forsake us. Hebrews 13:5.

D. We will be prepared and preprayered for the day's activities by being alone with God.

E. Jesus set an example for us. Even after He had a long tiring day, He got up before dawn the next morning to be with His Father alone. Mark 1:35.

II. HOW WE SHOULD USE
OUR TIME ALONE WITH GOD

A. First of all, this should not be a time of preparing a Bible study lesson or looking up answers to someone else's problem. This is primarily a time to nourish your own soul and to be concerned with your fellowship with God, not to worry about anyone else's spiritual condition. You cannot truly help anyone else unless God has first strengthened you. John 15:4-5.

B. Spend time in God's Word, meditating upon it and allowing Him to teach you from it. Begin by asking Him in prayer to speak to you and to open your heart to His Word. Psalm 119:9-11; II Timothy 3:16-17. For some suggested methods of study, see the outline "Bible Study: Growing in God's Word."

C. Spend time with the Lord in prayer. Prayer is the miracle we too often take for granted, for in prayer man communicates with the living God. Prayer is an exciting adventure into the heart and mind of God, and as such, it demands our most creative resources. Accordingly, a separate outline, "Prayer: Conversing with the Living God," is included. Here we merely make two suggestions.

    1. If your mind wanders while you're praying, pray out loud in a place where you can be alone with God. Many have found that the time spent driving to school or work can also be used for prayer. You, too, might find that your car makes a fine prayer closet! Matthew 6:6.

    2. Don't do all the talking. God is with you and He will teach you through His Word if you are open to Him. Psalm 94:12; John 7:17. Learn to be quiet with your mind and heart open to God for a period of time. Let Him bring thoughts to you as you wait upon Him. Be in an attitude of dependent awareness.

D. Some have found it helpful to record in a notebook what the Lord teaches them, including His promises and verses to memorize. Also, some write down what they pray for, so that they can better see God's faithfulness in answering prayer.

E. Spice up your time with variety; don't allow it to fall into a rigid pattern. Suggestions:

    1. Praise God by singing a hymn or two, as well as in prayer. Psalm 100:1, 2.

    2. Use a devotional book as an aid to getting into the Bible (e.g. *This Morning with God*, by Inter-Varsity Press).

    3. Memorize and later (e.g. while driving to school or work or while washing the dishes at home) meditate upon a verse or passage of Scripture. Psalm 119:11, 15.

    4. Make a list of people, past events, present circumstances, and future prospects you are thankful for, and thank God for each person or item on the list. I Thessalonians 5:17, 18.

    5. Read biographies of Christian men and women (e.g. missionaries) who have had a close walk with Christ.

III. GETTING STARTED

A. Select a time of day to be alone with God every day. We always allow time for meals, so how can we ignore time for our spiritual food? I Peter 2:2, 3. Many prefer the morning, as it focuses their eyes on God and prepares them for the rest of the day. Others are much more alert in the afternoon or evening and consequently spend time alone with God then. You must find the time of day that is best for you— give God your best time. Of course, there is nothing to prevent you from also spending some other time alone with God for a deeper Bible study or a longer prayer time.

B. There is no absolute maximum or minimum amount of time we should spend alone with God. If you're new at this, you may want to start with 10 minutes a day. Work up to a longer time if you find yourself desiring to spend more time in God's Word and in prayer. Psalm 104:34.

C. Decide upon a quiet place where interruptions are minimized. However, don't resent interruptions, even if it means postponing your time alone with the Lord until later. God may use you in another person's life through an interruption in your time alone with Him. Romans 8:28.

D. Realize that it will not be easy: Satan and your own flesh will both make it hard for you to meet with God on a regular basis. Matthew 26:41. If the morning is your chosen time, go to bed sufficiently early at night and ask the Lord to awaken you and make you alert in the morning. In addition, most people who select this time of day find it best to get out of bed and get dressed first, as the temptation isn't as great then to go back to sleep!

E. Don't get upset if you miss a day: the Christian life is life with another Person, Jesus Christ, and His love for you is not dependent upon whether you spend time alone with Him every day or not. For "you are not under law, but under grace." Romans 6:14. We don't spend time with God daily to earn His blessing; rather, we want to spend time alone with Him daily because of the grace He has lavished upon us. John 1:16. If we keep this in mind, then disciplining ourselves by making this a daily habit is honoring to God and profitable for our own lives as well. I Timothy 4:7, 8; Hebrews 12:11.

3

BIBLE STUDY: GROWING IN GOD'S WORD

I. INTRODUCTORY REMARKS

A. The word "Bible" comes from the Greek word "biblos," which means "book." Jesus called it "the Scriptures." John 5:39; Matthew 22:29. Paul referred to it as the "Holy Scriptures." Romans 1:2.

B. "Testament" means "covenant." The Bible is divided into the Old and New Testaments, which contain, respectively, God's covenants with man before and after the coming of Christ.

C. The Old Testament, which was written mostly in Hebrew over a span of about 1000 years, consists of 39 books.
  1. 5 Law (Pentateuch)—Genesis-Deuteronomy
  2. 12 Historical—Joshua-Esther
  3. 5 Poetical—Job-Song of Solomon
  4. 17 Prophetical
     a. 5 Major prophets—Isaiah-Daniel
     b. 12 Minor prophets—Hosea-Malachi

D. The New Testament, which was written entirely in Greek during the first century A.D., consists of 27 books.

  1. 4 Gospels—Matthew-John

  2. 1 Historical—Acts

  3. 21 Letters (often called epistles)—Romans-Jude

  4. 1 Prophetical—Revelation

E. There are many different versions of the Bible in English, some of which are more literal translations of the original texts in the original languages than others. Among the more literal translations are the New American Standard, Revised Standard, and King James versions. Among the paraphrased versions are J.B. Phillips, Good News for Modern Man, The Living Bible, and The New English Bible. It is generally considered to be best to use one of the more literal translations for Bible study and to use the paraphrased versions as sources for possible interpretations of the text.

II. INSPIRATION AND AUTHORITY OF THE BIBLE

A. *God's* Word

  1. Self-authentication of the Bible—Scripture itself claims to be the inspired Word of God: "All Scripture is inspired by God (literally, 'God-breathed') and profitable for teaching, for reproof, for correction, for training in righteousness; that the man of God may be adequate, equipped for every good work." II Timothy 3:16, 17. Of course, in itself this proves nothing, but a book which did not make this claim about itself would give little prospect of being the Word of God.

    a. The phrase "Thus says the Lord," or its equivalent, occurs over 2000 times in the Old Testament.

    b. David (II Samuel 23:2), Isaiah (Isaiah 8:1, 5, 11), Jeremiah (Jeremiah 1:9), Ezekiel (Ezekiel 3:4), Micah (Micah 3:8), and other Old Testament writers all claimed that their words and writings were inspired by God.

c. Peter claimed that the Old Testament was written by men moved by the Holy Spirit. Acts 1:16; I Peter 1:10, 11; II Peter 1:20, 21.

d. Paul considered the Old Testament to be the oracles of God. Romans 3:2.

e. At the beginning of many of his letters, Paul calls himself an apostle, sent not by men but by God. Moreover, he claimed to have received from the Lord what he preached. I Corinthians 11:23; Galatians 1:1, 11-12.

f. Peter regarded Paul's writings as part of the Scriptures. II Peter 3:15, 16.

g. John claimed to have written Revelation by the authority of God. Revelation 1:1.

2. Testimony of our Lord Jesus Christ—Jesus clearly taught the *complete* authority of the Bible as the Word of God. It has been well said that Scripture is the Word of the Lord and Jesus is the Lord of the Word. *We cannot accept Christ's Lordship over our lives without also accepting the inspiration and authority of the Bible.*

a. Christ taught that no part of the Law or Scripture can be broken or discarded. Matthew 5:17-19; Luke 16:17; John 10:34-35.

b. Christ explicitly labeled the Law of Moses as the Word of God. Mark 7:6-13.

c. Christ believed in and accepted the Old Testament. John 5:39; Luke 24:44.

d. Christ used Old Testament Scripture to answer Satan (Matthew 4:4, 7, 10; Deuteronomy 8:3; 6:16; 6:13, respectively) and men (Matthew 22:29-33, 43-46; Exodus 3:6; Psalm 110:1, respectively).

e. Christ indicated that He planned that His teachings would be written down later. Matthew 24:35.

f. Christ promised His disciples that after His departure the Holy Spirit would indwell them to guide them into all the truth, to disclose to them what was to come, and

22

to bring to their remembrance all that He said to them, thereby authenticating beforehand their teachings in the New Testament. John 14:26; 16:12-15.

    g. Christ revealed Himself supernaturally to Paul after His ascension (Acts 9:3-6; 22:6-10; 26:1-20; I Corinthians 15:7-9) and gave him authority to witness for Him (Acts 26:15-20).

B. Inspiration of the Bible

    1. What it is—Scripture has a double authorship: through the initiative and enlightenment, and under the superintendence, of God the Holy Spirit, each human writer of the Bible wrote what God wanted him to write and was kept from error in so doing. The Bible is at the same time *both* fully human and fully divine, just as was the Living Word, our Lord Jesus Christ, when He was on earth.

    2. What it is not

        a. The Bible is not inspired in the same way as the novel of a Hemingway or as the music of a Bach was inspired.

        b. Biblical inspiration does not mean that all of the ideas mentioned in the Bible are directly from God. For example, the words of evil men and Satan are not the words of God but are nevertheless recorded in the Bible by God's intention and inspiration.

        c. The inspiration of Scripture does not mean that the human writers of the Bible were essentially machines through whom God dictated. Their different personalities and writing styles are very evident in Scripture.

        d. However, Biblical inspiration does not stop with the human authors of Scripture, but extends to the finished product itself. They did not distort the truth they had been given in the process of writing it down.

        e. Biblical inspiration applies only to the text as originally produced by the writers. There have been some errors in copying through the centuries, but New Testament scholars tell us that putting all the variants of any consequence together would produce about one half of a page of copy and would not change any of our doctrines.

C. Interpretation of the Bible

    1. The fundamental principle for the interpretation of the Bible is that Scripture is to be read in context and interpreted in accordance with the overriding purpose(s) which the author had in writing. We must never jerk a verse out of its context, and that means not only its immediate verbal context in the book in which it appears but also the wider context of time, geographical setting, and human situation to which it belongs. Moreover, often the meaning of a verse or passage becomes clear when we study it in the light of other statements in Scripture on the same subject. As Oscar Cullmann points out, "The fountainhead of all false Biblical interpretation and of all heresy is invariably the isolation and the absolutizing of one single passage." God never contradicts Himself.

    2. Biblical interpretation is not a matter of having to join either the "literal" or the "figurative" camp: some parts of the Bible are to be taken literally, while other parts are to be taken figuratively. The crucial question is: What did the writer intend his readers to understand? When the psalmist declares that "the floods clap their hands" and "the hills sing for joy together" (Psalm 98:8), he is clearly speaking figuratively. But even a casual examination of Mark 6:30-44 shows us that Mark intended us to accept Christ's feeding of the 5000 as literal fact. Jesus assures us that the Holy Spirit will guide us into all the truth as we study diligently God's Word and submit to Christ's Lordship. John 16:13.

    3. In *Know What You Believe*, Paul Little suggests several useful principles regarding alleged errors in the Bible.

        a. The Bible speaks in phenomenological language, i.e. it describes things as they appear to be rather than in precise, up-to-date scientific terminology. To say that the sun rises in the east is an example of such a phenomenological statement. The Bible does not claim to be a science textbook—that's not its purpose—but neither does it give misinformation where it touches scientific matters.

b. Biblical information is not incorrect by virtue of its being incomplete. John admits to the selectivity of his gospel record. John 21:25. His leaving out events in Christ's life that were recorded by the other gospel writers does not prove that he or they were wrong.

c. We must guard against making the Bible say things which it really doesn't say. In particular, we must determine whether, in a particular instance, the Bible is speaking literally or figuratively.

d. Often a supposed conflict between Biblical teaching and scientific facts is merely a conflict between an interpretation of Scripture and an interpretation of scientific data.

e. To assume that the Bible is wrong where there are points of conflict would be foolish: the Bible has not changed in 1900 years, but scientific knowledge is ever-changing. To have reconciled the Bible to scientific views 100 years ago would have made Scripture obsolete today. Instead, we ought to admit the existence of apparent conflicts and await the development of additional evidence.

D. God's *Complete* Word

1. Many religious sects today, such as the Christian Scientists, Mormons, and Jehovah's Witnesses, justify their existence by claiming that they have received a revelation from God which is more recent and therefore superior to what is found in the Bible, so the question of whether God has given any further revelation since the days of the apostles is of practical importance.

2. Our answer to this question must be found in the Bible

25

itself. Jude, in verse 3 of his letter, appeals to us to "contend earnestly for the faith which was *once for all* delivered to the saints." This was the faith set forth by the apostles, as verse 17 indicates. Jude wrote this between A.D. 80 and 90, when all of the apostles except John had died or passed out of the picture, and was thus claiming that beyond the teaching of the apostles, no further revelation from God was to be expected.

3. Furthermore, Jesus Himself made it clear that the apostles' teaching was to be final and normative for His Church throughout all generations up to His return. In His prayer in John 17, He said, "I do not ask for these alone, but for those also who believe in Me through their word," thereby asserting that all of us who have lived since the apostolic age have only the apostles' words as our source for the knowledge of Jesus. The Bible, then, is God's complete Word to mankind.

E. The Only Infallible Rule of Faith and Practice

   1. Not only is the Bible *an* infallible rule, but it is also *the* infallible rule. The primary basis for this statement is II Timothy 3:16, 17, where Paul asserts that the man of God, having the inspired Scriptures, is "adequate, equipped for every good work." Scripture is the objective standard by which all subjective opinion is to be measured and tested.

   2. This assertion is not meant to imply that all other books are useless. Books have value insofar as they set forth knowledge that man attains from his investigations and reasonings about the world around him. However, only the Bible is God's revelation of vital knowledge which we could never gain by ourselves, and hence it is our sole infallible guide for living.

   3. There are two common objections to this declaration of the uniqueness of the Bible.

      a. *Objection*: Since men come to many conflicting interpretations of the Bible, a human referee (usually one or more officials of the church) is needed to settle these differences and establish the true interpretation.

Answer: The Bible does not encourage this idea of a human referee's deciding what it means. This makes tradition or human reason the source of religious authority, instead of the Bible. On the contrary, Luke in Acts 17:11 commends the Berean Christians for their placing even the apostle Paul, who was their teacher, under the control of the Old Testament by receiving "the word with great eagerness, examining the Scriptures daily, to see whether these things were so." If we discipline ourselves to think the Bible's thoughts after it, rather than our own, then much of the disagreement over interpretation will vanish.

b. *Objection*: Words and sentences are an inadequate means for God to use in revealing Himself; God has revealed Himself, not in Scripture, but in Jesus Christ. Every Christian comes to know God through a personal encounter with Jesus. The Word of God, then, is not the Bible but the revelation of Christ to His Church at any given moment.

Answer: Every Christian does indeed have a knowledge of God through Christ, the Living Word, made available to him by the Holy Spirit, but all knowledge of Christ which comes in this mystical way must be controlled by Scripture. God's self-disclosure is by deed *and* by word: He has revealed Himself in Jesus Christ, the divine witness to which is the Bible. The Bible is the one and only basis for our assurance that our conclusions from our personal encounter with the Lord are from the Holy Spirit, and not from our imaginations.

III. WHY WE SHOULD DILIGENTLY READ AND STUDY THE BIBLE

A. As we have seen, the Bible is God's complete revelation to

27

us, and *He wants us* to read and study it and to abide by the principles of living He has set forth for us in it. Scripture is to be our place of communion with Him, and one major reason for His sending us His Holy Spirit was that we might perceive the truths of the Bible.

B. Reading and studying His Word daily *reminds us* of His continual presence in our lives and of the fact that we are not "finished products" but rather "goods in process," i.e. that we *are being* conformed to the character of our Lord Jesus Christ.

C. God has established the reading and studying of His Word as *His way of equipping us* "for every good work" and of revealing to us His will for our lives. Paul wrote in II Timothy 3:16 that the Bible is profitable for four things— teaching, reproof, correction, and training in righteousness. Through His Word, then, God molds us into the mature Christian men and women He wants us to become.

IV. HOW TO GROW IN THE WORD OF GOD

A. *Begin with prayer*—Ask the Holy Spirit to open your heart and mind to the truths God wants to reveal to you in His Word. Psalm 119:18; John 16:13. This is honoring to God and places you in an attitude of dependent awareness and expectancy before Him.

B. *Read* the Word—I Timothy 4:13; Nehemiah 8:1-8.

C. *Study* the Word—Studying God's Word is *hard work* which requires discipline. The Holy Spirit will guide us into the truth only as we commit our mental capacities and energy, as well as our will, to Him. II Timothy 2:15. Just as the Christians in Berea did, we must examine the Scriptures daily and with great eagerness. Acts 17:11. In the next section we offer several possible methods of studying the Bible which are designed not to enslave you to them but to free you to discover more of God's truth.

D. *Memorize* the Word—The key to understanding the Bible is replacing our thoughts and mode of thinking with God's. A

28

very useful, and Scriptural, way of gaining this ability is by memorizing complete passages of Scripture (e.g. I Corinthians 13; James 1:2-8; or Galatians 5:13-26). It's important that we memorize key verses, too, but that generally is not as effective in helping us to learn to think God's thoughts after Him as memorizing a chunk of His Word. Psalm 119: 11; Deuteronomy 11:18; Proverbs 7:1-3.

E. *Meditate* on the Word—In addition to committing a portion of Scripture to memory, we must also be meditating upon it, as a cow chews her cud. Psalm 1:2; Joshua 1:8. Routine chores like washing dishes or daily activities like driving to and from work or school may provide excellent opportunities for reviewing a passage you're memorizing and for visualizing what it is that God is saying to you in the passage.

F. *Obey* the Word—Scripture teaches that obedience is the prerequisite of further enlightenment. Intellectual knowledge of the Word without obedience is useless. Matthew 13:11-12; James 1:22-25. It has been well said that "light obeyed increases light, but light rejected brings night."

G. *Spread* the Word to others—The best way to learn anything is to teach it to someone else. Moreover, we are commanded to share with others what God has revealed to us. Matthew 10:32; Acts 1:8; Hebrews 5:12. We, like Paul, should make it our purpose in life to proclaim Jesus Christ, "admonishing every man and teaching every man with all wisdom, that we may present every man complete in Christ." Colossians 1:28, 29. God has constructed us in such a way that we find joy in life as we do so.

V. POSSIBLE METHODS OF PRIVATE BIBLE STUDY
A. Book study (inductive approach)
   1. Read
      a. Choose one of the 66 books in the Bible and read it through entirely—preferably in one of the more literal translations (e.g. the New American Standard, Re-

vised Standard, or King James). If you have done little or no reading in the Bible in recent years, you might find the gospel of John or Paul's letter to the Romans to be good places to start.

b. If applicable, next write a brief paragraph summarizing the historical situation.

c. Try to list the major purpose(s) of the book—why was it written?

d. Starting at the beginning of the book again, divide up the book into smaller passages for study.

2. Study

    a. *Observation*—Read the passage carefully. What does it *say*? What are the main facts (who, what, where, when, why, and how)? Is this passage part of a progression of ideas? Look for repeated words as an index to what the author considered important. Watch for connectives and contrasts and other keys to the thought structure. What style is the writer employing, and why?

    b. *Interpretation*—What does the passage *mean*? Look up the meanings of key words in a dictionary. What figures of speech are used by the writer, and what do they mean? Why is this particular word, phrase, or idea used? Why is it placed here by the writer? How does this idea fit in with the rest of the passage? Finally, what are the implications of these statements? Beware of spiritualizing: don't let your desire to illustrate familiar truth keep you from discovering fresh truth. Look up the cross-references to tie in your study of the passage with the rest of Scripture.

    c. *Application*—What does the passage *mean to me*?

        (1.) First apply the main point to your life. Is there an example to follow, a command to obey, a promise to claim, or a gift to be thankful for? What requires a change of thought? How can I make that change? What requires a change in my behavior? What action must I take now? What will I need sometime in the future?

    (2.) Next apply any other meaningful point in the passage to your life.

    (3.) Make your applications concrete by considering how this passage relates to your attitudes toward God, yourself, and others in your family, other Christians, your employer and fellow employees, etc.

    (4.) Finally, apply your will to God's will, and thank Him for teaching you through His Holy Spirit.

3. Reread (optional)—Rereading the entire book after completing the passage-by-passage study may give you a far greater feeling for the continuity of the book and open up new insights for you. This is particularly helpful in studying one of the Gospels or Acts, which may take several months or more.

B. Gospel study (Matthew-John)

The same principles suggested for the book study apply here as well, but there are also several specialized questions that can lead to fresh insights from the Gospels. We are indebted to Chuck Miller for these "filters" through which he passes every paragraph in all of the Gospels:

1. In this paragraph, *who* initiated the situation and *how* did he or they do it? Sometimes Jesus did; on other occasions others came to Him first.

2. What is the *major* aspect of Christ's concern for people here—physical, mental, social, emotional, or spiritual?

3. What is the response to Christ in this incident—positive, negative, or not recorded?

4. What is the level of Jesus' ministry here—one-on-one, small group, or large group?

5. What phase of leadership is occurring here? Phase 1: Jesus does it; phase 2: Jesus does it, and His disciples are with Him; phase 3: Jesus' disciples do it, and He's with them; phase 4: Jesus' disciples do it, and He's way in the background encouraging them.

6. What are the disciples learning through this incident? Or, what is it that they could, but may not, be learning? Be specific in your list.

7. How are the disciples learning this? Or how are they being discipled by Jesus? It may be by listening to and observing Him, by asking Him questions, or by serving others, for example.

8. What can *you* learn from this incident for your own life today? About Jesus Christ? About yourself? Others?

This approach is particularly helpful in revealing to us our Lord's *methods* of evangelism and discipleship training, which can and should be readily applied to our own lives and circumstances.

C. Epistle study (Romans-Jude)

Again, the same principles suggested for the book study apply here, but there are some additional ideas for letters only that might be helpful.

1. Paragraph titles—After reading the letter through for the first time, divide it up into paragraphs by its content and find a one- or two-word title for each paragraph. This will give you a basic overview of the letter's structure and will aid you in recalling its essential contents.

2. People—Next jot down on a sheet of paper everything you can find out, verse by verse, about the major characters in the letter, including the author and person(s) to whom the epistle was addressed. Of particular value is historical data, not general theological material. To use Paul's short letter to Philemon as an example, divide a sheet of paper into three columns as follows:

Paul	*Philemon*	*Onesimus*
V.1 prisoner of Jesus Christ; not alone— with Timothy.	V.1 beloved brother and fellow-worker of Paul's.	V.10 converted by Paul while Paul was in jail.
V.4 thankful for	V.2 lives with	V.11 formerly

Paul	_Philemon_	_Onesimus_
Philemon's love and for his faith toward Jesus and all the saints.	Apphia (wife?) and Archippus (son?); there is a church in his house.	useless; now useful to both Paul and Philemon V.12 is being sent back to Philemon; is Paul's very heart.

3. Historical situation—From this information, write a brief paragraph summarizing the situation. To illustrate this, we again use Paul's letter to Philemon: Philemon, a Christian and probably a businessman and large estate owner, had a slave, Onesimus, who had apparently robbed him before running away to Rome. There Onesimus met Paul (perhaps through Timothy), who led him to Christ while in jail. Paul, who had apparently led Philemon to the Lord previously, returned Onesimus to him with this letter.

4. Purpose(s)—Next list the major purpose(s) of the letter. Our assumption is that the New Testament letters are not random notes written for no particular reason. What is the author's specific reason(s) for writing? Paul's letter to Philemon is essentially a plea to Philemon for leniency in regard to Onesimus, for runaway slaves, when caught, were generally disfigured or killed. Paul was trying to help Philemon integrate his social, economic, and spiritual lives by applying the love ethic to a real-life situation.

5. Strategy—Now go back over the entire letter again, verse by verse, jotting down _how_ the author seeks to accomplish the major purpose(s) you just listed. Why does Paul mention the facts that he does? How does he organize them to achieve his purpose(s)? Why does he use the particular language and words that he does? What theological points about the nature of God, man, sin,

33

salvation, etc. are made, and how do they help to achieve the writer's objective? We turn again to Philemon: *Verse 1*—By calling himself a "prisoner" rather than an "apostle" or a "bond-slave" of Christ as he does elsewhere in his letters, Paul identifies himself with Onesimus (who had broken the law and thus deserved, from a purely legal point of view, to be punished) and underplays his authority as an apostle (see vv. 8, 9). Timothy's inclusion in the salutation implies that he may have known Philemon and could have carried some weight, too. Philemon is affirmed by Paul and placed on an equal plane with him in preparation for Paul's appeal. *Verse 2*—Paul includes others in the salutation to point out that Philemon is not an independent agent but is functioning in a community of believers. Our moral decisions have an influence on others, and Paul is very subtly reminding Philemon of this. Paul identifies himself with Archippus, too ("fellow-soldier").

6. Application—Now carry on with the crucial cultural and personal application stage, as in the book study method in general.

D. Topical study

Choose a topic of importance and trace the topic through Scripture.

1. Examples—The outlines in this book are examples of topical studies. Another example is a study of Paul's view of Jesus Christ, as expressed in his letters in our New Testament. As you accumulate material, you might classify it according to these subtopics: His names, His attributes, His Deity, His humanity, His sufferings and death, His resurrection, and His second coming. Biblical terms and doctrines (e.g. faith, justification, grace, and prayer) also make fruitful topical studies.

2. Study aids

   a. Concordance—an alphabetical list of all the important words in the Bible, with references to the passages in which they occur. If your topic is actually a word appearing in Scripture, a concordance is extremely helpful in directing you to the appropriate places in Scripture.

b. Bible dictionary—a dictionary of the people, places, books, and doctrines of the Bible. Recommended: *The New Bible Dictionary*, edited by J.D. Douglas, William B. Eerdmans Publishing Company, 1962.

c. Topical Bible—a digest which groups every Bible verse related to a given topic under a suitable heading, often printing out the verses in full. Recommended: *Nave's Topical Bible*, Orville J. Nave, Moody Press.

E. Biographical study

Nearly 3000 people are mentioned in the Bible, and the lives of many of them make interesting and profitable biographical studies. Carefully examining the lives of Biblical figures and the ways God deals with them can reveal much about God's character and about how He deals with *us*. Using a concordance or topical Bible, look up every reference to the person you're studying. Questions you might want to consider include the following:

1. What did he accomplish during his life?

2. Did he face a major crisis in his life? If so, how did he face it?

3. Does his life display any development of character?

4. What was his experience with God?

5. Did he display any particular faults?

6. Is there any outstanding sin in his life? What factors led up to his committing this sin? How did it affect the rest of his life?

7. Is there any lesson in his life that is outstanding to you? Example: Gideon (Judges 6-8).

VI. MISTAKES TO AVOID

A. Don't "pick and choose" the sections of Scripture you are going to read or believe or put into practice. If you do, you

NOW LET'S SEE... CLOSE THE EYES, OPEN THE BIBLE, POINT THE FINGER...

are depending on your own subjective, imperfect judgment rather than on God's objective, omniscient judgment. The Bible does not merely *contain* the Word of God; it *is* the Word of God—all of it!

B. On the other hand, don't *worship* the Bible. Its central purpose is to exalt the Living Word (Jesus Christ), not itself, so we want to be worshipping Him as we study it. John 20:31.

C. In going to the Bible for guidance on specific matters, don't take verses out of context. We can "make" the Bible say just about anything we want it to if we do. The absurdity of the "close-the-eyes, open-the-Bible, point-the-finger, and read-the-verse" approach is clearly seen in this amusing story: A young man seeking the Lord's will for his life closed his eyes and opened his Bible to Matthew 27:5: "Judas went away and hanged himself." Not particularly delighted by this, he tried again, and read Luke 10:37: "Go and do likewise." Determined to make one more valiant effort, the young man closed his eyes and turned to John 13:27: "What you do, do quickly."

D. Don't allow human philosophies to pervert your thinking. Studying them may be of value to you, but continually submit your mind and heart to God's Word as you are doing so. Colossians 2:8.

E. Don't neglect the importance of Christian fellowship in the Word to a proper, balanced understanding of the Bible. God wants us to meet with Him alone, but we also need to be part of a body of believers that meets regularly for Bible study so that God can through them correct any faulty conclusions we may inadvertently draw from our private study of the Word. Moreover, we need to listen frequently to men gifted by God in teaching from His Word.

F. Bible commentaries can be a very useful aid in studying Scripture, particularly in supplying needed background information, but don't rely on them to do your digging into the Word for you. Many prefer to look at a Bible commentary only after they have completed all of the phases of study themselves. Recommended one-volume commentary for the entire Bible: *The New Bible Commentary: Revised*, Inter-Varsity Press, 1970.

G. Don't approach the Bible with only your mind, but with your emotions and will as well. If you leave out the application stage in studying Scripture, you will be denying God the privilege of equipping you for all that He has in store for you.

H. Don't regard disciplining yourself in your study of God's Word as in any way incompatible with being open to the leading and teaching of the Holy Spirit. Although it is true that there is such a thing as over-disciplining ourselves and thereby stifling the Spirit, He definitely wants to teach us through our disciplining our heart and minds in the study of Scripture. Solomon exhorts us to seek insight "like silver and search for it as for hidden treasures." Proverbs 2:4.

I. At the same time, don't get upset if a day passes without your reading the Bible. "You are not under law but under grace." Romans 6:14. We don't read His Word to earn His blessing; rather, we want to read His Word daily because of the grace He has lavished upon us. John 1:16. If we keep this in mind, a daily study of the Bible glorifies God and is profitable for us as well. I Timothy 4:7, 8; Hebrews 12:11.

VII. BIBLIOGRAPHY

A. Campus Crusade for Christ. *Ten Basic Steps Toward Christian Maturity*, Step 5—"The Christian and His Bible," 1968.

B. Little, Paul. *Know What You Believe*. Scripture Press Publications, 1970.

C. Nyquist, James. "Leading Bible Discussions." Inter-Varsity Press, 1968.

D. Pinnock, Clark. *Biblical Revelation*. Moody Press, 1971.

E. Richards, Lawrence O. *Creative Bible Teaching*. Moody Press, 1970.

4

PRAYER:
CONVERSING
WITH THE *LIVING* GOD

I. BASIC PRINCIPLES
A. *What* Prayer Is
1. In the Bible, prayer is seen as two-way communication with the Living God. Prayer is thus speaking and listening to God. As such, it is the highest activity of which the human spirit is capable. Too often, it is also the miracle we take for granted.
2. Prayer is trust active, "faith in action." Even waiting upon God for His answer is not a passive experience, but rather an exciting adventure into the heart and mind of God which demands all of our resources.

B. *Whom* We Are to Pray to
1. We are to pray *to* God the Father. Matthew 6:6, 9; Ephesians 3:14; Philippians 4:6; Colossians 1:12.
2. We are to pray *through* (Romans 1:8) and *in the name of* Jesus Christ, God the Son (John 14:13; 15:16; 16:23). Through Christ, our Mediator (I Timothy 2:5) and our Advocate before the Father (I John 2:1-2), we have

access to the Father. Romans 5:1-2; Ephesians 3:11-12.
To pray in the name of Christ is to recognize His
authority over our lives and to claim His authority before
the Father.

3. We are to pray *in* the Holy Spirit. Ephesians 6:18; Jude
20. Paul explains what this means in Romans 8:26-27:
Since we are blinded by our sin and consequently do not
know how to pray as we should, the Holy Spirit inter-
cedes for us and for other Christians, according to the
Father's will. Prayer is thus offered to the Father, in the
name of the Son, and by the inspiration of the Holy
Spirit, who is resident in every believer from the moment
of his conversion.

C. *Why* We Are to Pray

1. Jesus commands us to pray. Matthew 6:6, 9; Luke 18:1.
Paul also urges prayer. Philippians 4:6; Colossians 4:2; I
Thessalonians 5:17-18.

2. We have specific needs—physical, mental, social, emotional, and spiritual—that God can and will meet as we
lay them before Him, for He is our Heavenly Father who
is ready to give what is good to those who ask Him.
Matthew 7:7-11.

3. Others have specific needs for which we are to pray.
James 5:16.

4. The fundamental reason why we are to pray, however, is
that the prayers of those who seek to carry out His will are
a delight to God. Proverbs 15:8. Insofar as we are filled
with gratitude to Him for giving us His Son, in order that
we might begin now to experience a taste of the abundant life that will be ours for eternity (John 10:10), we
will want to converse with Him in prayer.

D. *When* We Are to Pray

1. At all times—I Chronicles 16:11; I Thessalonians 5:17. As
we go about our day's activities, we are never alone: the
Christian life is life with another Person, Jesus Christ.
Prayer "without ceasing" is an *attitude* of dependence

upon Him rather than an *act*. Someone once said, "Prayer is to spiritual life what breathing is to physical life." As we grow to know Christ better, we will keep our channels of communication open to Him on a more continual basis, regardless of what else we may happen to be doing at the time.

2. Specific occasions—examples
   a. Before meals, we are to thank the ultimate Provider. Mark 6:41; 8:6-7; 14:22-23; Acts 27:35; Romans 14:6; I Corinthians 11:24.
   b. In times of crisis, we are to commit the crisis, and ourselves, to His all-encompassing wisdom, love, and sovereignty. Psalms 18:6; 107:6; Jonah 2:1-2; Acts 4:23-30; 12:1-12.
   c. When important decisions need to be made, we are to look to our Father for His guidance. Luke 6:12-16; Acts 1:21-25.
   d. On a regular (at least daily) basis, we are to spend time alone with the Lord in prayer.

3. In addition, at *any* time the Holy Spirit within us wants to pray.

E. *Where* We Are to Pray
   1. In private—inside (Matthew 6:6) or outside (Mark 1:35). The mountains were a favorite place of prayer for our Lord. Mark 6:46; Luke 6:12.
   2. With other Christians (Matthew 18:19-20; Acts 16:25; 20:36).
      a. In God's House (Mark 11:17; Acts 3:1).
      b. In private homes (Acts 1:13-14; 12:12).
      c. Outside (Acts 21:5).

   See IV below for suggestions concerning group prayer.

F. *How* We Are to Pray
   1. The Lord's Prayer (or, more appropriately, the "Disciples' Prayer") is our Lord's guide for us. Matthew 6:9-13; Luke 11:2-4. His emphasis is on praying for *God's* will to be accomplished. Matthew 6:10.

2. In addition, there are dozens of prayers in the Bible that have much to teach us about how to pray. For example:

   a. Solomon's prayer of dedication for the Temple—I Kings 8:22-61.

   b. King Hezekiah's prayer for deliverance from the King of Assyria—II Kings 19:14-19.

   c. Ezra's prayer after hearing of Israel's mixed marriages in violation of God's commandment to Israel—Ezra 9:5-15.

   d. Psalms

     (1.) Personal prayers for healing (6), pardon (51), protection (57), communion (63), and vindication (109), as well as personal prayers of praise (103).

     (2.) Formal "sanctuary" prayers of praise (100,150).

   e. Daniel's prayer for a rebellious Israel—Daniel 9:3-19.

   f. Jesus' prayers during the final week before His crucifixion

     (1.) High Priestly Prayer—John 17.

     (2.) Garden of Gethesemane prayer—Mark 14:32-42.

   g. Jerusalem Christians' prayer after the release of Peter and John by Jewish authorities—Acts 4:23-30.

   h. Paul's prayers in his letters to churches—Romans 1:8-12; Ephesians 1:15-19; 3:14-19; Colossians 1:9-12.

Note: In many of the appeals in these prayers, God is urged to defend *His* name by fulfilling the request of His people, "so that all the peoples of the earth may know that the Lord is God." I Kings 8:60.

3. In His parables and other teachings Jesus urged:

   a. Persistence in our prayerful requests—Luke 11:5-8; 18:1-8 (the unrighteous judge). The Greek verbs in Jesus' oft-quoted promise in Matthew 7:7 are in the continuous present tense: "*Keep asking*, and it shall be given to you; *keep seeking*, and you shall find; *keep knocking*, and it shall be opened to you."

   b. Humility and repentance in prayer—Luke 18:10-14 (the Pharisee and the publican).

    c. Prayer offered in a forgiving spirit—Matthew 18:21-35 (the unjust servant).

    d. Sincerity in prayer—Matthew 6:5, 6.

    e. Simplicity in prayer—Matthew 6:7; Mark 12:38-40.

    f. Intensity in prayer—Mark 14:38.

    g. Unity in prayer—Matthew 18:19.

    h. Expectancy in prayer—Mark 11:24.

4. We turn now from our discussion of internal attitudes in prayer to make several observations concerning external factors in prayer.

    a. Prayers may be spoken aloud or not, as we wish and as circumstances permit. In group prayer, praying aloud makes possible fellowship in prayer. In private prayer, praying aloud may help prevent the wandering-mind problem and tends to keep us more alert to the Holy Spirit's leading. However, in the classroom or on the job, our prayers may have to be silent ones.

    b. The use of "King James English," with its "Thees" and "Thous," is neither required nor prohibited. The prayers in the Bible were prayed in Hebrew and Greek. Pray in terms *you* feel comfortable using. God is not interested in your trying to learn a new jargon to converse with Him.

    c. There is no single authorized "prayer position" in the Bible. We may drop to our knees (Ephesians 3:14; Isaiah 45:23; Philippians 2:10), or bow our heads and close our eyes, or stand up and lift our eyes up to heaven (Mark 6:41; John 11:41; 17:1). In fact, we may want to pray in all of these and other positions at one time or other in our Christian experience.

II. ELEMENTS OF PRAYER—A-C-T-S

A. Adoration—Since prayer springs out of our love for God and our longing to worship Him, what better way to begin our prayers can there be than to acknowledge His worthiness of our praise? Specifically, we can praise Him for His infinite wisdom, all-encompassing love, and creative power. Matthew 6:9. Examples: I Kings 8:23-24; Psalms 63:1-5; 103; Daniel 9:4.

B. Confession—

1. We cannot be genuinely worshipping God for His greatness for long without being overcome by a profound sense of our own inadequacy. Sin is not confined to our *acts* but extends to our *omissions* (Luke 10:29-37— parable of the good Samaritan), and especially to our *motives* (Matthew 6:1-8).

2. As the Holy Spirit reminds us of a sin which we have committed, we should admit before God our *specific* offense, acknowledge that we come to Him with no excuses, thank Him for His forgiveness of the sin through Christ, and repent of (i.e. turn away from) the sin. Matthew 6:12; I John 1:9. James urges us, in addition, to confess our sins to other Christians. James 5:16. Confession of our sins brings immediate forgiveness from God, for Christ nailed them to the cross. Colossians 2:13-14; Romans 8:1-2.

C. Thanksgiving—We are urged by Paul to rejoice and thank God *in*, and moreover, *for*, all circumstances. I Thessalonians 5:18; Ephesians 5:20. Even if, in regard to a particular circumstance, we don't *feel thankful*, we can and should nevertheless *give thanks*, and, at the same time, ask God to change our attitude. Philippians 4:6; Colossians 4:2. Examples of thanksgiving in prayer: Psalm 30:2-3; John 11:41-42; Romans 1:8; I Thessalonians 1:2-10.

D. Supplication—In the context of our adoration, confession, and thanksgiving, God *wants* us to make *specific* requests of Him, both for our own needs (Matthew 6:11-13) and for those of others (James 5:16), including our political rulers (I Timothy 2:1-2) and those who persecute us (Matthew 5:44). There are at least three reasons why this is God's will for us.

1. God loves us and is ready to give what is good to us. Psalm 84:11; Matthew 7:7-11; James 1:17.

44

2. Such requests are a testimony to the world that we believe in God's loving nature and in His ability to meet all of our needs—physical, mental, social, emotional, and spiritual.

3. As God answers our specific requests, our faith in Him is increased, and we are enabled to dare to commit more of ourselves to Him.

For examples, see III below.

III. DOES GOD *REALLY* ANSWER PRAYER?

A. There are dozens of promises in the Bible that God answers the prayer requests of those who come before Him in sincerity and obedience. Our Lord, in particular, made quite a number of such promises to His disciples. Matthew 7:7; 18:19; Mark 11:22-24; John 14:13-14; 15:7,16; 16:23.

B. There are hundreds of instances in the Bible of specific requests which were fulfilled by God to the letter. Examples: Abraham's request for a son (Genesis 15:1-6; 21:1-3); Gideon's request for signs of God's power (Judges 6:36-40); Elijah's pleas for no rain for three years, and then for rain (I Kings 17:1, 7; 18:1, 42-45; James 5:17-18); Daniel's intercession for Israel (Daniel 9:16-23); Peter's request that Tabitha be restored to life (Acts 9:40).

C. Nevertheless, all of us who have ever prayed know that God does not *always* fulfill our specific requests just as we ask them. The apparent rejection of some of our requests, in the face of the Bible's promises, often produces doubt concerning God's faithfulness in answering prayer or concerning our own standing with Him. It is to this serious problem that this section is devoted.

D. The promises of the Bible concerning prayer must not be interpreted apart from the many examples in Scripture of answers to prayer which were not in precise fulfillment of the verbalized request.

1. Answers to prayer *delayed*: Psalms 22:1-2; 40: 1; Jeremiah 42:7; Habakkuk 1:2; Luke 18:7; II Peter 3:8-9.

45

2. Answers to prayer *exceeding the petition*.

   a. Solomon asked for wisdom and received wisdom, riches, honor, and long life. I Kings 3:7-14; II Chronicles 1:10-12.

   b. The Jerusalem Christians prayed for Peter in prison; God's answer included Peter's miraculous deliverance from prison. Acts 12:5-16.

3. Answers to prayer *different from the request*.

   a. Moses asked to be allowed to cross the Jordan; God's answer was permission to view the land of promise. Deuteronomy 3:23-27.

   b. Paul prayed three times that the "thorn in his flesh" be removed; God's answer was a promise of grace to endure it. II Corinthians 12:7-9.

   c. Martha and Mary came to Jesus with an appeal for their sick brother Lazarus. Jesus delayed for several days, in spite of His love for Lazarus, and by the time He arrived at their home, Lazarus had died. But Christ raised him from death, thereby inducing many of the Jews who had observed this to believe in Him. John 11:1-45.

E. Most of Jesus' promises regarding our petitions in prayer contain the important stipulation that our requests be *in His name*, and this stipulation can probably be inferred in the others. To ask for something in the name of another person is to ask in accordance with his will, on his behalf, and just as he himself would do it.

F. Conclusions

   1. Accordingly, there is no magical formula in prayer that guarantees that our specific requests will be granted in the exact way that we ask them. God *does* answer prayer, but His answer may be no. And even if His answer is yes, it may not come as soon as we may think it should, or in the precise way that we may have requested. The perfect will of God for our lives and for all of creation, not what

46

we in our limited wisdom think is best, determines His answer to our prayers. I John 5:14-15.

2. More specifically, God answers our prayers not necessarily by giving us precisely what we ask for, but rather by giving us what we *would* ask for if: (1) we knew, as He does, what is really best for us in the long run, and if (2) we were 100% willing to live for Him, rather than for ourselves. Only if we had infinite knowledge and an unconditional willingness to carry out God's will for our lives at all times could it be any other way. Nor would we really want it any other way. Martha and Mary were rather bitter about Lazarus' death when Jesus finally arrived, but there can be no doubt that a little later they would have agreed that Jesus' answer (raising Lazarus from death in the presence of some of the hitherto unbelieving Jews) was far greater than a literal fulfillment of their request would have been. In the face of apparent rejections of our specific requests, we need the "Lazarus perspective" that will enable us to have faith that: (1) God knows better than we what is best for us, and that (2) *someday* we too will know why granting this particular request of ours was not best for us.

3. Consequently, when we bring our requests to God, we recognize that we are coming before Him not to change His mind but to have our minds changed by Him. A helpful analogy is that when a person comes to a dock in a boat, he doesn't pull the dock to the boat, but rather pulls the boat to the dock.

4. Nevertheless, the fact that our requests may not always turn out to be in God's perfect will does not imply that we should be in any way hesitant or reluctant to bring them before Him. Like an umpire in baseball, we "call them as we see them." We are consistently urged by the New Testament authors to draw near to God with confidence and with faith. Philippians 4:6; Hebrews 4:16; 10:22; 11:6; James 1:5-7. We are to pray boldly and specifically

47

for needs as they arise, but at the same time we are to be alert for God's answer in any of a number of ways and to praise Him for it.

IV. GROUP PRAYER
A. Scriptural Precedent for Group Prayer
  1. Our Lord's promise in Matthew 18:19-20: "If two of you agree on earth about anything that they may ask, it shall be done for them by My Father who is in heaven. For where two or three have gathered together in My name, there I am in their midst."
  2. The early church's example—Acts 1:13-14; 2:42; 12:12; 16:25; 20:36; 21:5.
B. Benefits of Group Prayer
  1. Christ promises answers to those who meet and agree on prayer requests in His name. Matthew 18:19-20.
  2. By praying for others *in their presence*, we express our love for them, and close bonds of friendship develop readily. Warning: Don't pray *only* for those who are absent!
  3. Group prayer alerts us to the needs of others in times of crisis. We cannot "love one another" if we don't know one another's needs.
  4. Group prayer fosters honesty in our relationships with others, so that differences may be recognized and reconciled before they are allowed to grow to the point where permanent scarring will result.
  5. Group prayer helps us sense God's presence *at all times*.
  6. By praying aloud in a group that accepts us *as we are*, we learn to accept ourselves and are liberated from the fear of others.
  7. Group prayer helps us recover the nearly lost art of listening to others without interrupting them.
  8. Group prayer, conversing with God in the presence of others who know Him, makes talking about God with others who *don't* know Him considerably easier.

C. Dangers of Group Prayer

  1. "Performance prayer"—Beware of "playing to the crowd" in group prayer, i.e. praying to impress others in the group. Matthew 6:1, 5-6.

  2. "Preaching prayer"—The purpose of group prayer is to converse, together, with *God*; using a time of prayer to preach to others in the group is manipulative and is a very unacceptable substitute for confronting them directly.

D. Suggested Guidelines for Group Prayer

  1. Meet at some place (usually a home is best) where outside distractions are minimized.

  2. Sit in a circle so that each person can see everyone else in the group.

  3. To bring the group together in preparation for the time of prayer, open with a brief message from Scripture prepared by one of the group members or with a time of sharing God's answers to past specific prayer requests. Creative leadership is a valuable asset here.

  4. In sharing needs with the group, make requests personal and specific, yet brief.

  5. Encourage the soft-voiced members of the group to hold their heads up and project when they pray. We can't agree on a prayer request that we can't hear!

  6. Encourage brief prayers, for only one request at a time, so that others can conveniently add their own words of agreement to the request if they so desire. The prayer meeting is not the place for long-winded, all-encompassing pastoral prayers. Such prayers, in succession, often tend to become quasi-competitive, rather than supportive, and also tend to put everyone else to sleep! Encourage those who have an abundance of prayer requests to pray many times, but only for one request at a time.

  7. Don't be afraid of brief periods of silence: prayer is listening, as well as speaking, to God.

  8. Keep the meeting moving; don't get bogged down on

one particular need unless a majority of the group is actively involved in the discussion and/or prayer. Moreover, don't allow the meeting to drag on too long. There is no quicker way to effect a drop in attendance next week. If you notice several people glance at their watches, you've probably gone too long already. It is far better to have them leave wanting more.

9. If there are a number of people who aren't accustomed to praying aloud in a group, after some needs have been shared, break up for prayer into groups of three or four so that everyone can participate without embarrassment. If *you* are reticent about praying aloud in a group, work yourself up to it gradually. Start by getting alone with God daily and praying out loud. If you feel that you don't know what to say, read—*out loud*—some of the great prayers in the Bible (see I.F.2. above) for some ideas. Then find a Christian who is more comfortable praying in a group situation and pray with him or her as regularly as possible. In prayer, just as in any other endeavor, practice fosters confidence. It is ironic that often those who find it hardest to pray in the presence of others have no difficulties whatever in *talking* with the same people. Remember that prayer is addressing the God who is *always* with us! So relax, and pray simple prayers. You *can* do it!

E. Bibliography

Rinker, Rosalind. *Praying Together* and *The Art of Conversational Prayer*. Zondervan.

V. MISTAKES TO AVOID

A. Don't regard prayer as a substitute for other available forms of action. Be prepared *and* preprayered!

B. Don't be too quick to assume that a particular set of circumstances is necessarily God's final answer to your prayer. Keep alert to the continued leading of the Holy Spirit, and subject any apparent answers to the objective test of conformity to the Bible. God will not lead you to do anything which He enjoins in His Word.

C. Don't let a busy schedule crowd out prayer. It is said that before a busy day, Martin Luther used to devote an *extra hour* to prayer.

D. Don't regard prayer as a burdensome responsibility to God, but as a priceless privilege, an open invitation to come into His "study" to converse with Him at any time, for any reason.

5

FELLOWSHIP:
THE GIFTS OF THE HOLY SPIRIT
FOR THE BODY OF CHRIST

I. FELLOWSHIP IN THE BODY OF CHRIST

A. When we become Christians, we immediately become part of the Church, i.e. the body of all believers in Jesus Christ. I Peter 2:9; Ephesians 1:22-23. When Jesus Christ calls us to Himself, He calls us to each other simultaneously. An isolated Christian is accordingly a defeated Christian. It is our privilege and our duty to meet with others in God's family to worship Him, to study His Word, to pray, to celebrate the Lord's supper, and to move out together into a lost world, ministering hope and love. Hebrews 10:23-25; Ephesians 4:15-16; Romans 12:4-6.

B. The term "fellowship" has in some circles become so watered-down that it is applied to any gathering of people for any purpose. However, "koinonia," the Greek word which we translate "fellowship," was used in the first century to denote *closeness* in association. "Koinonia" was accordingly a favorite term for the marital relationship as the most intimate between human beings. It is this term that Luke uses to describe the fellowship of the early church in Acts 2:42.

C. In several of his letters, Paul uses the analogy of the human body to describe more fully the character this "koinonia" is to have. Romans 12:4-5; I Corinthians 12:12-27; Ephesians 4:15-16.

  1. There are many members, but one body. All the members do not have the same function. Yet every member has a useful function, and every member is to some degree dependent upon every other member, although he will obviously be most directly affected by those nearest to him. Just as our physical bodies are not healthy unless each individual part is functioning properly—our feet as well as our hands, and our ears as well as our eyes—so also "the proper working of each individual part" of the body of Christ is essential to "the growth of the body for the building up of itself in love." Ephesians 4:16.

  2. Consequently, there can be no feelings of inferiority or superiority within the body of believers. For "God has placed the members, each one of them, in the body, *just as He desired*" I Corinthians 12:18. Rather, Christians are to be so entangled in caring for one another that when "one member suffers, all the members suffer with it," and when "one member is honored, all the members rejoice with it." I Corinthians 12:25-26.

D. The agent of this unity is the Holy Spirit: "By *one* Spirit we were *all* baptized into *one* body, whether Jews or Greeks, whether slaves or free, and we were *all* made to drink of *one* Spirit." I Corinthians 12:13. The Holy Spirit, sometimes referred to as the "Silent Member of the Trinity" because He bears witness to Jesus Christ and not to Himself (John 16:14), is God the Father's gift to us at the moment we trust in Christ for our salvation. Romans 8:9. Like the Father and the Son, the Holy Spirit is a Person, not a mere substance, force, or concept—a "He," not an "It." He has a will (I Corinthians 12:11), an intellect (Romans 8:27), and emotions (Ephesians 4:30), just as we do. Paul describes the Holy Spirit as God's "down-payment," or "pledge," or "first installment" to us. II Corinthians 1:22; 5:5; Ephesians 1:14. He lives within us permanently as God's assurance to us that He will save us, as He has promised. God the Father is Creator (Genesis 1:1); God the Son, Redeemer (Romans 3:24); and God the Holy Spirit, Sanctifier (Romans 15:16; I Peter 1:2). To "sanctify" means to set apart as holy for the work of God. Several ways the Holy Spirit is sanctifying us are by convicting us of our sins, by teaching us the meaning of God's Word, and by bringing things to our remembrance. John 14:26; 16:8-15.

E. In addition to this *gift* of the Holy Spirit (viz. the Holy Spirit Himself), there are *gifts* of the Holy Spirit, which are a vital element in our fellowship with other believers, and it is to this aspect of His ministry that the remainder of this outline is devoted.

II. SPIRITUAL GIFTS—BASIC PRINCIPLES

A. The main Biblical passages are Romans 12:1-8; I Corinthians 12-14; Ephesians 4:7-16; and I Peter 4:10-11.

B. Spiritual gifts are capacities for service to the body of Christ. One or more of these gifts is given by the Holy Spirit to each Christian at the time of his spiritual rebirth. The Apostles Peter and Paul teach clearly that every believer has received *at least* one gift, for note the words "each one" in the following verses: I Peter 4:10; I Corinthians 12:7, 11; Ephesians 4:7. As God is generous in all His giving, it is not unusual for individual Christians to possess several gifts. However, some gifts lie dormant and undiscovered for years, and probably no one knows all of his gifts at the start of his walk with Christ.

1. Spiritual gifts are related to, but must be distinguished from, natural talents. Both are gifts from God (James 1:17) and both are to be developed by the person entrusted with them. Moreover, both may (and should) be used to serve Christ. But natural talents, such as a special athletic or musical ability, are given by God to Christians and non-believers alike, while only Christians are given spiritual gifts, for they and only they are indwelt by the Giver of spiritual gifts, the Holy Spirit.

2. The *gifts* of the Spirit must also be distinguished from the *fruit* of the Spirit in that fruit (love, joy, peace, patience, kindness, goodness, faithfulness, gentleness, and self-control) is what the Holy Spirit wants to produce in *every* believer, while no individual Christian has all of the gifts. (If he did, he wouldn't need anyone else in the body of Christ! I Corinthians 12:29-30.) Fruit refers to the formation of Christian character; gifts relate to ways of serving others. Galatians 5:22, 23.

C. The Greek word which we translate "spiritual gifts" ("charismata") literally means "grace-gifts." We don't merit or earn spiritual gifts by anything we do, just as we don't merit the grace (i.e. undeserved favor) by which we have been saved. Ephesians 2:8-9. The Holy Spirit distributes gifts "to each one individually *just as He wills.*" I Corinthians 12:11. This rules out all boasting and all competition regarding gifts.

D. Spiritual gifts are given for the purpose of building up the body of Christ in love and equipping God's people to do the work of ministering life and truth in the world. I Corinthians 12:7; Ephesians 4:11-13; I Peter 4:10. They are not intended for mere personal use.

E. Spiritual gifts can be abused by being employed in the power of the flesh. II Timothy 1:6, 7. We must yield ourselves to God to minister our gifts in the power of the Holy Spirit. Romans 12:1, 2. The evidence of the proper use of the gifts by the individual Christian is the manifestation of love to God and to the other members of the body of Christ. Such love, the "more excellent way" (I Corinthians 12:31), puts the gifts to their proper uses, and without love the gifts are useless. I Corinthians 13:1-3.

III. WHY YOU SHOULD SEEK TO DISCOVER YOUR GIFT(S)

A. Obligation to God—God has not given you gifts for you to be ignorant of them and not exercise them. Paul teaches that we are each responsible to discover, develop, and exercise our spiritual gifts. I Corinthians 12:1; I Timothy 4:14. Moreover, why would he list various gifts in several of his letters if we were not to discover our own gifts? Don't be like the unfaithful servant of Jesus' parable in Matthew 25:14-30 who fails to make good use of the resources his master entrusted to him. The following objection is often voiced: "If I am in the will of God, why do I need to know what my spiritual gifts are?" The answer is that exercising our spiritual gifts is an essential aspect of being in God's will.

B. Obligation to self—God has so constructed us that we find true joy only when we are serving Him, and one indispensable way we serve Him is by serving others in His "forever family." You should thus *enjoy* exercising your spiritual gifts for the good of the body. Moreover, we move toward our ultimate goal (Christ-likeness—Ephesians 4:13) only as we are serving others. Thus, the discovery and proper exercise of your spiritual gifts will result in your own spiritual maturity.

C. Obligation to other Christians—*You* are an indispensable and unique part of the body of Christ. Others need you to exercise your spiritual gifts; if you don't, their spiritual growth may be dwarfed.

IV. THE GIFTS

There are two general categories of spiritual gifts—speaking

56

gifts (ministry of the Word) and serving gifts (ministry of service). I Peter 4:11. The list of gifts that follows *may* not be exhaustive, for Paul offers us two different, partial lists in Romans 12 and I Corinthians 12. However, these gifts are certainly representative of the gifts given by the Holy Spirit to the body of believers as a whole.

GIFT	PURPOSE	DESCRIPTION
Prophecy Romans 12:6 I Cor. 12:10, 14:3	Proclamation of divine revelation	The capacity to reveal God's will to others for the future (foretelling) and/or for the present ("forthtelling").
Teaching Romans 12:7	Instruction	The capacity to communicate truth clearly with wisdom given by the Holy Spirit; clear and accurate interpretation of Scripture.
Faith I Cor. 12:9	Enabling	The capacity to see a need and to believe that God will meet it: vision.
Wisdom I Cor. 12:8	Insight	The capacity to make practical application of

GIFT	PURPOSE	DESCRIPTION
		truth in God's Word to concrete situations.
Knowledge I Cor. 12:8	Understanding	The capacity to systematize truth in God's Word.
Discernment of spirits I Cor. 12:10	Protection	The capacity to distinguish between what is from God (truth) and what is a deception wrought by Satan (error).
Mercy Romans 12:8	Manifestation of love to the "undeserving"	The capacity to demonstrate sensitivity to human need with Holy Spirit-inspired acts of love.
Exhortation Romans 12:8	Strengthening	The capacity to provide consolation, encouragement, and motivation to carry out God's will.
Giving Romans 12:8	Advancement of God's work	The capacity to give material resources with liberality and cheerfulness.

GIFT	PURPOSE	DESCRIPTION
Leadership Romans 12:8	Direction	The capacity to preside and to set the direction of a project in a way that aids the spiritual growth of others.
Administration I Cor. 12:28	Organization	The capacity to organize and make efficient use of the resources of the body of Christ.
Service Romans 12:7 I Cor. 12:28	Service	The capacity to serve the physical needs of the body of Christ in a way that strengthens others spiritually.
Healing I Cor. 12:9, 28	Restoration	The capacity to heal the sick, by the power of God, in response to the Holy Spirit-given faith.
Miracles I Cor. 12:10, 28	Special signs	The capacity to be God's instrument in accomplishing the supernatural.

GIFT	PURPOSE	DESCRIPTION
Tongues I Cor. 12:10, 28	Personal edification	The capacity to speak in a language one has never learned.
Interpretation of tongues I Cor. 12:10	Aid to the gift of tongues	The capacity to translate utterance in tongues by Holy Spirit-given revelation.

V. COUNTERFEITS OF THE GIFTS

Paul begins his discussion of the gifts of the Spirit in I Corinthians 12 with a basic reminder of the Lordship of Jesus Christ (verses 1-3). The use of the gifts must always be subject to Him. When this is not done, what is displayed is a *fleshly* or *Satanic* counterfeit of the gift. Fleshly counterfeit is reliance upon oneself; Satanic counterfeit is inspired by the Devil. An example of the former is relying solely on oratorical ability, emotional appeals, or human wisdom apart from the Holy Spirit in preaching the Gospel. I Corinthians 2:1, 4. An example of the latter is teaching false doctrines under the inspiration of evil spirits. There are many false teachers around today, as Paul predicted would happen. I Timothy 4:1. Protect yourself from them and the serious problems they can cause you by getting into the habit of evaluating, on the basis of conformity or noncon-formity to God's Word, all teaching that you receive. II Timothy 3:16, 17. (Start with this outline!)

VI. THE MINISTRIES AND OFFICES

A. A ministry is the sphere in which one exercises his spiritual gifts. This sphere may refer to a certain group of people, as Peter was sent to the Jews while Paul was sent to the Gentiles. Galatians 2:7,8. Or this sphere may refer to a certain geographical area, as God calls some of His children to a ministry on a foreign mission field but wants others to live for Him in their home country.

B. Every believer is to take part in at least one basic ministry by using the gifts the Spirit has given him. I Corinthians 12:4-6.

C. We are called purely by grace to our ministry. Ephesians 3:7. However, the church is to recognize and endorse that ministry. Acts 13:1-3.

D. Certain offices, which represent the institutionalization of some of the gifts, were appointed by Christ for the functioning of the local church. Ephesians 4:11, 12.

    1. Apostle—an eyewitness to the resurrection of Christ who plants churches. I Corinthians 9:1; Acts 1:21-26; Ephesians 2:19, 20. There are thus no apostles today. Instead we have the inspired writings of some of them in the New Testament.

    2. Prophet—one who gives forth God's Word to the church at large. There are many varieties of this gift, and all believers are urged to seek after it because of its great importance. I Corinthians 12:28; 14:1.

    3. Evangelist—one who proclaims the gospel to the unsaved and then gathers new believers together as an assembly of the body of Christ to instruct them in God's Word. In this sense, the evangelist is a church planter, a missionary responsible for establishing the church in unevangelized regions.

    4. Pastor-teacher—one who sees to it that the church is functioning properly (e.g. that the members are being cared for and that discipline is exercised when needed) and who teaches truth and wisdom clearly from God's Word. I Corinthians 12:28. The spiritual gift of teaching which some, but not all, believers are given and the office of pastor-teacher to which some, but not all, believers are called must be clearly distinguished from the responsibility we all have to "let the word of Christ richly dwell" within us, "with all wisdom teaching and admonishing one another." Colossians 3:16. The author of Hebrews reproves his readers for not yet being teachers. Hebrews 5:12. The distinction seems to be that the pastor-teacher is responsible for teaching and caring for his flock of believers individually *and* collectively, while other Christians generally teach one another individually or in small groups. A special warning against spiritual pride accompanies the call to the office of pastor-teacher. James 3:1. The pastor-teacher is often also called an elder, bishop, or shepherd. The Bible sets down some requirements for a would-be elder and also lists some of his responsibilities. Titus 1:5-9; I Peter 5:1-5.

5. Deacon—one who is held responsible for the caring ministry of the church, and particularly the physical needs of the believers. In the New Testament church this meant serving tables. Acts 6:1-7. Among the first deacons was the first Christian martyr, Stephen. Luke implies that the deacons were instrumental in the growth of the early church in Jerusalem because they freed the twelve apostles to devote themselves to prayer and to the ministry of the Word. Acts 6:7. The requirements for a deacon are set down by Paul in I Timothy 3:8-13.

E. Not every believer is appointed to an office, and all such appointments are purely by God's grace.

VII. HOW TO DISCOVER *YOUR* GIFT(S)

A. Knowledge—Study the various passages relating to the gifts of the Spirit so that you will not be ignorant of them. I Corinthians 12: 1. To further increase your knowledge, read a book or listen to others teach on this subject.

B. Prayer—Ask the Lord to show you ways in which you can serve the body of believers of which you are a part. Notice that this presupposes that you are in a functioning community of believers who are endeavoring to serve Christ. See I.A.

C. Reflection—Reflect on your past and present ministries.

I JUST CAN'T SEEM TO FIND MY SPIRITUAL GIFTS!

Among the gifts you have tried to exercise:

1. Which ones have you enjoyed?

2. Which ones have been recognized and appreciated by others in the body of believers?

3. Which ones appear to be most needed in the body right now?

4. Which ones appeal to you as ways in which you might be able to build up the body of believers?

D. Experimentation—Experiment by trying out various gifts in your present ministry, as opportunities arise.

E. Counsel—Seek the counsel of mature Christians who know you well. Ask them what gifts they have observed in you and in what areas God has used you most.

F. Assessment—Prayerfully evaluate your competence in the gifts you think the Holy Spirit has given you. Don't expect immediate perfection; look for improvement and development.

G. Conviction—Seek to use the gifts you feel you have in the power of the Holy Spirit, i.e. by faith. If these are not your gifts, God will let you know in due time. If they are and if you operate in the power of the Spirit, God will honor this by affirming you in your use of these gifts.

VIII. MISTAKES TO AVOID

A. Don't regard your search for your spiritual gifts as a game, but rather as an important matter which will directly affect how faithful you are in serving Christ by serving His body.

B. Don't fail to serve the body of believers in areas other than where you feel your chief gifts lie. Our aim should always be to build up the body of believers in *whatever* ways we can, and our motive, love for Christ and His body. It is no coincidence that each of the four passages on the gifts of the Holy Spirit (Romans 12:6-8; I Corinthians 12,14; Ephesians 4:7-13; I Peter 4:10-11) is immediately preceded or succeeded by a passage on the indispensability of love. Romans12: 9-21; I Corinthians 13; Ephesians 4:14-16; I Peter 4:8-9.

C. Don't take extreme positions that are not taught in Scripture, such as believing that all speaking in tongues or all miracle-working is Satanic or that every true Christian speaks in tongues or leads people to Christ every week.

D. Finally, don't seek the gifts as ends in themselves. Seek the One who gives us His Holy Spirit and His gifts, the Lord Jesus Christ. Get to know Him better and learn to operate in the power of the Spirit by faith. The gifts are given to build up the body of Christ and to move that body out into the world, i.e. they are given to be given. Since "it is God who is at work in you, both to will and to work for His good pleasure," you should enjoy and find challenging and rewarding the exercise of your gifts. Philippians 2:13.

IX. BIBLIOGRAPHY

A. Dolphin, Lambert. *The Church Is Alive*, Good News Publishers, 1971.

64

B. Hay, Alex Rattray. *The New Testament Order for Church and Missionary.* New Testament Missionary Union, 1947.

C. Stedman, Ray C. *Body Life.* Gospel Light Publications, 1972.

6

THE CHRISTIAN
AND
SPIRITUAL LIFELESSNESS

I. NATURE OF THE PROBLEM

A. God's will for all of us is that we experience—now and eternally—an abundant, fruitful, and joyous life based upon a personal, ever-growing relationship with His Son and our Lord, Jesus Christ. John 10:10; 15:5, 11; 17:3; I Corinthians 2:9.

B. As we grow into spiritual maturity, our lives begin to display:

1. An increasing hunger for and understanding of God's Word. Hebrews 5:12-14; Acts 17:11.

2. A greater desire to praise and thank God for who He is and what He is doing. Colossians 3:16,17; I Thessalonians 5:18.

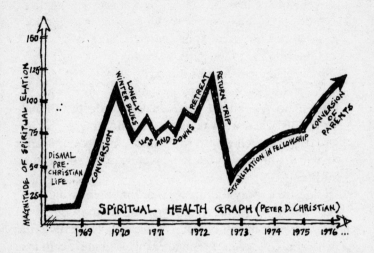

SPIRITUAL HEALTH GRAPH (PETER D. CHRISTIAN)

Labels on the graph: DISMAL PRE-CHRISTIAN LIFE, CONVERSION, LONELY WINTER BLUES, UPS AND DOWNS, RETREAT, RETURN TRIP, STABILIZATION IN FELLOWSHIP, CONVERSION OF PARENTS

Vertical axis: MAGNITUDE OF SPIRITUAL ELATION (25, 50, 75, 100, 125, 150)

Horizontal axis: 1969 1970 1971 1972 1973 1974 1975 1976 ...

3. An eager anticipation of what the Lord has for us *today*. Psalm 118:24.

4. A greater desire for meaningful fellowship ("koinonia") with other Christians. Hebrews 10:24,25.

5. A greater faithfulness in prayer on behalf of others. James 5:16; John 17, especially vv. 9, 20.

6. A more effective outreach for the Lord to non-Christians. I Thessalonians 1:8; Acts 1:8.

7. Greater evidence of the fruit of the Holy Spirit (e.g. love, joy, peace, patience, kindness, goodness, faithfulness, gentleness, and self-control—Galatians 5:22,23) who lives within us and empowers us to live as we ought to.

C. However, Christians at *all* levels of spiritual maturity occasionally experience periods of spiritual lifelessness or stagnation. These periods may last for only five minutes, or they may last for years. Some Christians are susceptible to greater "highs" and "lows" than others, and thus exhibit more dramatic changes in their spiritual health, but *all* Christians do at times experience lifelessness, which may be marked by one or more of the following symptoms:

67

1. No desire to read the Bible, which may seem to us to be merely an academic exercise irrelevant to our needs.
2. No desire to praise or thank God—what was formerly reality for us may now be merely clichés. We can try reading Psalms to test ourselves here.
3. No eager anticipation of the day's activities, but rather the "blah's" or perhaps even bitterness over what we have to do. A good index is often our *first* fleeting thought or feeling when we wake up in the morning.
4. No desire for fellowship with other Christians, the value of which may seem to us to lie merely in the social realm of life.
5. No desire to pray for ourselves or for others, which may seem to us to be merely a psychological exercise.
6. No desire to share the wealth of the gospel of Jesus Christ with non-Christians. Personal evangelism may seem to us to be hypocritical and perhaps even to be an interference with the personal right of others to hold their own beliefs.
7. Moral "backsliding," the spoiling of the fruit of the Holy Spirit starting at our weakest point. How important is it to us that we are in the process of being conformed in character to Jesus Christ?
8. Doubts set in—about God's faithfulness to us, perhaps even about His existence, and/or about the sincerity of our commitment to Him. "Has God *really* said . . . ?"—the serpent (Genesis 3:1).

D. These symptoms, coupled with our knowledge of the fact that we ought to be happy as we are serving the Lord, may create a conflict within us. Whether we are conscious of it or not, our failure to be able to reconcile God's perfect will for our lives (our theology) with our lifelessness (our reality) becomes a growing source of frustration for us.

E. The tragic results of unchecked spiritual lifelessness are always present on two different levels.
   1. Individual—We may withdraw from honest, personal fellowship with other Christians, preferring to hibernate

in our shell of stagnation, where our style of life drops to a lower plateau which seems more comfortable to us.

2. Corporate—What is often overlooked by us is that the entire body of believers in Jesus Christ, and especially the local fellowship of which we are a part, is weakened by *our* spiritual lifelessness. When "one member suffers, all the members suffer with it." I Corinthians 12:26. Just as a healthy human body has all of its parts functioning properly, i.e. carrying out its particular responsibilities, so also our exercising our particular spiritual gifts and talents within the community of believers is essential to the community's well-being. I Corinthians 12:7,12.

II. THE GENERAL SOLUTION

A. The solution to the problems which our periods of spiritual lifelessness bring lies not in *our* efforts to restore ourselves to life but rather in God's nature, as the Expert Exploiter of Evil. God did not want Adam to sin, but ever since he did, God has been exploiting evil for His own good purposes. The greatest example of this is the paradox of the crucifixion, which in one sense is the supreme tragedy of history (the violent death of God's only begotten Son at the hands of godless men) and yet which three days later was revealed as the supreme victory of history (the means to our salvation and new life—now and eternally—with God). Acts 2:22-24.

B. Consequently, although periods of spiritual lifelessness are not part of God's *perfect* will for us, He nevertheless wants to exploit them, when they do occur, to build us into the mature Christians He wants us to become. If God were to bring us out of our lifeless periods immediately, all by Himself, we would miss out on the growth which God can bring about in us and also on the experience of community which can result from mutual problem solving. But most importantly, we would fail to learn to seek *Him* persistently. Luke 11:5-10; Mark 10:46-52. Paul writes in Romans 8:28: "And we know that God causes ALL (not 'a few' or 'some' or even 'many') things to work together for good to those who love God." We need to learn to see even a fraction of the potential for good that God sees in our periods of lifelessness.

C. Our general strategy when we find ourselves in a period of spiritual lifelessness is thus:

1. Rejoice, and thank God for it. We are urged by Paul to thank God *in* all circumstances and, moreover, *for* all circumstances. I Thessalonians 5:18; Ephesians 5:20. Moreover, we have seen that God wants to exploit this state of affairs for good (specifically, to make us more like Jesus Christ), so we can thank Him in advance for what He is going to teach us and do in us through this period of lifelessness and through our response to it. This is the key step and probably the one most often neglected.

2. Then attempt to identify the cause(s) of the spiritual lifelessness.

3. Finally, take specific action designed to deal with the cause(s) involved.

We turn now to some examples of the application of this general strategy.

III. TEN CAUSES OF LIFELESSNESS, WITH CORRESPONDING SPECIFIC REMEDIES

A. *Cause*: Sin

A definite transgression of God's commandments which we refuse to admit or resisting the Lordship of Christ in an area of our lives (e.g. our money, our job, or our time) can result in a period of spiritual stagnation. Psalm 32:3, 4. See also the short book of Jonah.

Solution: Confession of specific sins

1. We can first thank the Lord for His gracious provision (His Son Jesus Christ) for all of our sins. Moreover, we can praise God for conviction of *specific* sins by the indwelling Holy Spirit, without whom we would continue in our sin unaware of the harm we are causing our

Heavenly Father, ourselves, and the body of believers. Hebrews 12:4-11.

2. Confession involves realizing the specific offense we have committed, admitting this offense to God, asking and thanking Him for His forgiveness, and repenting of (i.e. turning away from) the particular sin committed. Genuine confession of sin is simultaneously accompanied by the forgiveness of our sins, by our Lord's cleansing us of all unrighteousness, and by the renewed assurance of our forgiveness. I John 1:9. Christ nailed our sins to the cross, so that forgiveness of all our sins is an accomplished fact. Colossians 2:13, 14. The barrier of unconfessed sin is on our side—not God's—for He always loves and is ready to forgive us. Romans 8:1.

3. In addition, James urges us to confess our sins to other Christians. James 5:16.

B. *Cause*: Purposelessness

By no means restricted to the unemployed, unskilled man with no sense of where he is headed in life and no friends, lifelessness due to a lack of a meaningful purpose in an area of our life often hits even the successful businessman, his wife active in the local PTA, and their straight-A, athletic-star son in college. This lack of purpose may relate to something as little as what to do on a free Sunday afternoon or as great as what occupation to enter.

Solution: Setting personal goals and priorities

1. We can first thank God that He has a purpose for our lives not only in the future but also right now. Furthermore, inasmuch as we are not fulfilled if we aren't moving toward that divine purpose, our feelings of lifelessness are instruments of God's grace motivating us to discover and carry out God's perfect purposes for our lives.

2. Periodically we all need to spend several hours or more with the Lord in prayer evaluating and perhaps reformulating our goals in life—both general (long-term) and specific (short-term).

a. Throughout His earthly ministry, our Lord revealed His clear understanding of His primary goal in life, going to the cross in obedience to His Father to die for our sins. Mark 8:31; 9:12, 31; John 2:19; 10:11,15,18. He also had other goals which supported this main goal, such as healing the sick and training His disciples to carry on the work of the ministry after His ascension. Even a casual reading of any part of the gospels reveals Jesus' certainty about what He wanted to do.

b. Moreover, Jesus gave His disciples goals to work towards. For example, just before His ascension, He commissioned them to be His witnesses "both in Jerusalem (specific, short-term goal), and in all Judea and Samaria, and even to the remotest part of the earth" (general, long-term goal). Acts 1:8.

c. The Apostle Paul also had a very clear understanding of his primary purpose in life: "And we proclaim Him (Christ), admonishing every man and teaching every man with all wisdom, that we may present every man complete in Christ." Colossians 1:28.

3. Having set some goals based upon the teaching of God's Word and also upon the particular set of spiritual gifts and talents with which we have been entrusted, we then need to set our priorities in accordance with these goals. "The plans of the diligent lead surely to advantage, but everyone who is hasty comes surely to poverty." Proverbs 21:5. Are we "making the most of our time?" Ephesians 5:16. If we are in doubt about a certain priority, we can ask ourselves if it will count for eternity.

4. Setting general and specific personal goals and priorities should have several immediate advantages.

   a. We should find it easier to make decisions; God's will should be less elusive.

   b. As we achieve—by God's grace—our specific goals, this experience of success should encourage us to expect God to do greater things in and through us.

c. When we fail, we will be able to see clearly where and why we have failed, instead of merely having a vague feeling that somehow we have "let God down." Seeing our failures clearly is essential if we are to learn from them, claim Christ's forgiveness for them, and avoid repeating them.

C. *Cause*: Spiritual undernourishment

Just as our daily meals are vital to our physical health, our daily time in which we let God speak to us personally through prayer and the reading of His Word is indispensable for our spiritual welfare. We cannot give away what we do not have!

Solution: Motivation and discipline in Bible study and prayer

1. We can first thank the Lord for His desire to have fellowship with us at all times, in spite of our humble state, and for the great amount of trouble He had to go to in order that we today might have the Bible as His inspired Word to us. Since we continually need to be in personal fellowship with Jesus to be fulfilled in our humanity, we can also thank God for showing us by our feelings of spiritual stagnation when that fellowship is missing.

2. Discipline is worthless until we have first allowed God to rekindle our love for Him and our thirst for His righteousness. When this rekindling is necessary, making a list of what and whom we are thankful for, and then thanking God out loud for each item and person on the list can be very helpful. "In everything give thanks" is more than a commandment: it's also healthy advice! I Thessalonians 5:18.

3. However, once this is done we may still need practical help for a new discipline in our personal devotional lives. I Timothy 4:7, 8. If at all possible, we should first find a regular time and a quiet place for our daily devotions.

Suggestions for spicing up this time with the Lord include the following:

a. Praising God by singing a hymn or two as well as in prayer. Psalm 100:1,2.

b. Using a devotional book as an aid to getting into the Bible.

c. Jotting down in a notebook what God teaches us as we read.

d. Memorizing and later (e.g. while driving to work or school or while washing the dishes at home) meditating upon a section of Scripture that is particularly meaningful to us. Psalm 119:11, 15.

e. Reading biographies of Christians who have had a close walk with the Lord.

D. *Cause*: Loneliness

Adam and Eve's initial sin sent them scampering into the bushes to hide from God and from each other, and man has been in the bushes ever since. Genesis 3. Very possibly nothing can cause spiritual lifelessness to set in faster than loneliness, and in our computer-oriented society we perhaps have to face loneliness today more than ever before. Even men of God who are well-known church leaders surrounded by many Christians often confess being lonely. A lonely Christian is a defeated Christian.

Solution: Meaningful relationships with others

1. We can first thank God for creating us to be in relationships with others. He recognized that man in Genesis 2 needed a helper, other than God Himself, and so created woman that we might have relationships with other human beings as well as with our Creator. Then we can thank Him for the reminder of this perfect purpose for our lives that our loneliness can provide.

2. Meaningful relationships with others don't come easily for many of us. To start, we might find one person to interact with. Perhaps he will be someone who has already attempted—with little or no success—to get to know us better. Or he might be another lonely person. There are certainly plenty around from whom to choose.

3. A growing number of Christians today are finding great strength in small groups of believers who commit themselves to God and for a given period of time, to each other in certain, mutually agreed-upon ways. Often called "covenant communities," "think-and-pray groups," or "accountability groups," these small groups can, if they get beyond the superficial level, foster strong ties of love among the individuals in them. Acts 2:42-47.

E. *Cause*: "Christian ghetto-ism"

Many of us suffer from a lack of meaningful contact with non-Christians, evidently finding it more comfortable to stay within the safe confines of our circle of Christian friends than to venture to reach out to a non-Christian that God brings across our paths. But God created us in such a way that we need not only to take in spiritual food but also to give it out to others, or else stagnation may soon set in.

Solution: Confessing Christ before non-Christians

1. We can first thank the Lord that He has chosen to use us as His instruments to reach others with the message of His love for them. Once we begin to understand what a privilege this is, we can thank Him for fashioning us so that if we *don't* give out, *we* will give out!

2. We need to examine our lives to see where, if at all, there is significant contact with non-Christians. It may even be necessary for us to set some new goals and realign our priorities in accordance with our Lord's emphasis upon the importance of our confessing Him before others. Matthew 10:32,33; 28:18-20; Mark 16:15; Luke 24:45-49; John 20:21; Acts 1:8. Then we need to pray for and be alert for opportunities to share the good news of Jesus Christ with others who don't yet know Him personally.

F. *Cause*: Breakdown in personal relationships

God's will for us is right relationships with others, and any friction that exists between us and others may catapult us into a period of lifelessness. Scripture indicates that a clear conscience is a prerequisite for successful spiritual achievement. I Timothy 1:18,19. In his "Institute in Basic Youth Conflicts," Bill Gothard defines a clear conscience as "that inner freedom of spirit and assurance (which comes) from knowing . . . that no one is able to point a finger at you and accuse you of wrongs toward him that you have never made right." He points out that continuing to harbor bitterness not only grieves the Holy Spirit but also hurts us as well: since we are capable of only one emotional focus at a time, when we focus on hate toward another person rather than on love toward God, we tend to become like those we hate.

Solution: Reconciliation

1. We can first thank the Lord that we find true fulfillment only in that which is His will for us, i.e. in right relationships with others. Moreover, we can praise God for the gifts of conscience and of the Holy Spirit to enable us to see clearly our part in the breakdowns in our relationships so that healing can take place.

2. We are called to be ministers of reconciliation, i.e. to be people in the business of making enemies into friends, not only between man and God but also between man and man. II Corinthians 5:17-21; Matthew 5:9; Mark 9:50; Romans 14:19. God did not wait for us to come to Him to repent of our rebelling against Him; rather, while we were still helpless sinners, He sent His Son to die for us. Romans 5:6,8. As agents of reconciliation, we also must take the initiative in moving to the person with whom we have a conflict and seek to make things right again. "If possible, so far as it depends on you, be at peace with all men." Romans 12:18. We must go humbly, asking for forgiveness without offering excuses for our behavior. Matthew 5:23, 24. And as we have received forgiveness from God, we must freely forgive others who hurt us. Matthew 6:12-15; 18:21-35; Romans 12:17,19. This often results in a closer relationship with the person

than before the breakdown and provides one more illustration of God's exploitation of evil for good. Romans 8:28.

G. *Cause*: Spiritual overeating

A few Christians can seemingly take in an unlimited amount of spiritual food, but most, no less sincere, have a limited capacity to digest spiritual food. For example, a period of spiritual lifelessness often follows attendance at a fruitful Christian retreat.

Solution: Spiritual "fasting"

If this is our problem, we may want to limit our devotional lives to a minimum, pray short prayers, and cut down on Christian fellowship activities until the dry spell passes. However, if lifelessness persists, it may have another cause which requires a different response.

H. *Cause*: Spiritual overstrain

A heavy week of preaching sermons, leading Bible studies, or counselling may cause pastors or other Christian leaders to feel spiritually "wrung out."

Solution: Retreat

We may need a temporary change of environment and type of activity. Upon the return of Jesus' 12 disciples from their first preaching tour, Jesus had them go away with Him "to a lonely place and rest a while." Mark 6:30-32. Periodically we, too, need to retreat from our everyday surroundings to spend time alone with the Lord to be spiritually revived.

I. *Cause*: Neglect of our bodies

Our bodies, spirits, and souls are not independent entities: the lack of health of any one of them may adversely affect the others. Particularly common is spiritual lifelessness caused by the failure to give our bodies what they need.

Solution: Proper care of our bodies

Our *bodies*—not our spirits—are the "temples of the Holy Spirit." I Corinthians 6:19. Moreover, it is our bodies that Paul urges us to present as living and holy sacrifices to God.

Romans 12:1. One day we will all be trading in our present mortal bodies for imperishable models (I Corinthians 15:35-58), but for the present, God has given us the responsibility of taking care of our mortal bodies. Consequently, we must be certain that we are getting sufficient sleep and physical exercise. Sometimes our lifelessness is best combatted by putting on tennis shoes and running around the block as hard and fast as we can to clear out our cobwebs. A balanced diet with the vitamins we need is another must.

J. *Cause*: Loss of balance between work and rest
God's creation is based upon this balance. Genesis 2:3. Our neglect of it reveals our arrogance ("I don't need a rest, Lord!") and sooner or later weakens our creative spiritual forces, which leads to lifelessness.
Solution: Playful relaxation
We must learn to sense when we need to take time out to relax, to celebrate, to play games, or to absorb ourselves in a hobby. This may even prove to be a greater testimony for our Lord than pious seriousness, which may leave others in awe of us but will not bring them any closer to a relationship with Jesus Christ.

IV. MISTAKES TO AVOID

A. Don't automatically assume that unconfessed sin is the cause of your spiritual lifelessness. It might not hurt to check this out by prayerfully trying to recall your recent activites, but do not make the mistake of Job's friends who insisted that his misfortunes must have been caused by his sin. There are many other possible causes of spiritual lifelessness, and we have suggested nine above.

B. Consequently, don't be ashamed of spiritual lifelessness and definitely do not try to hide it from others behind an ever-ready, "victorious-life, Christian smile." That only grieves the Holy Spirit (the Spirit of *truth*—John 14:17) and erects additional barriers to honesty with others. Instead,

DON'T TRY TO HIDE SPIRITUAL LIFELESSNESS BEHIND A VICTORIOUS LIFE SMILE.

talk about your lifelessness with a mature, understanding Christian friend.

C. Don't fall into the trap of thinking that there is no hope of escape from the particular complications surrounding your spiritual lifelessness. However great they may seem to you, *God* can handle them. Matthew 19:26; Philippians 4:11-13. Moreover, His promise to us is that no temptation has overtaken us but such as is common to man, and that *He* is faithful and will not allow us to be tempted beyond what we are able to endure, and that with the temptation He will also provide the way of escape. I Corinthians 10:13. Try comparing your problems with Job's six-fold tragedy: his possessions were stolen and destroyed, his servants were killed, his sons and daughters were killed, his health was taken away, his wife turned against him, and his friends accused him of sin. In the face of all this, Job fell to the ground and worshipped, saying, "Naked I came from my mother's womb, and naked I shall return there. The Lord gave and the Lord has taken away. Blessed be the name of the Lord." Job 1:20, 21.

D. Finally, don't regard spiritual lifelessness as merely a sickness but rather as a symptom of recovery also: God's seeming far away can cause us to suffer only if at other times we have experienced His nearness. Suffering due to spiritual lifelessness is thus a sign that the Holy Spirit is present in us and contains the promise of new spiritual health.

V. BIBLIOGRAPHY

Trobisch, Walter. *Spiritual Dryness.* Inter-Varsity Press, 1970.

7

BAPTISM

I. BASIC PRINCIPLES
A. Old Testament parallels—the covenants

A "covenant," as the word is used in Scripture, is a guarantee by God of His faithfulness to His people. It is a legal relationship conceived, established, and revealed totally by His grace. Genesis 9:9. It is not to be regarded as a contract whereby God and man exchange promises, even though the recipients of the covenant have an obligation to abide by the terms of the covenant. Genesis 17:9-14. God established covenants in Old Testament times with Noah (Genesis 6:18; 9:8-17), Abraham (Genesis 12:1-3; 15:18; 17:1-8), Moses (Exodus 6:6-8), and David (Psalm 89:3-4, 26-37; 132:11-18). In the new covenant inaugurated by the death of Jesus Christ, the grace exemplified in preceding covenants was brought to its fullest exhibition. Mark 14:24; Luke 1:67,72; I Corinthians 11:25; Galatians 3:15-16; Hebrews 9:11-15.

1. Noahic covenant (I Peter 3:18-22)—Just as Noah and his family, secure in the ark, passed through God's judgment on sin in the form of a flood, so also the Christian, secure in Christ, will pass through God's future judgment on sin. John 5:24. Baptism here represents the establishing of a new covenant and our personal entrance into its benefits.
2. Abrahamic covenant (Colossians 2:11-12)—Just as circumcision was the sign and seal of righteousness for the Jew (Genesis 17:11; Romans 4:11), baptism is God's stamp of approval on the Christian.
3. Mosaic covenant (I Corinthians 10:1-2)—The Israelites' baptism "into Moses" was their passage through the Red Sea, symbolizing separation *from* the pagan Egyptians and *to* God. Baptism thus simultaneously points back to God's wondrous acts of deliverance and forward to a life of obedience to Him.

B. John's baptism
1. John's baptism called people to "repent" of their sins. Mark 1:4. True repentance is not merely a feeling of guilt or remorse but rather a 180° turn away from sin.
2. John himself contrasted his baptism with water for repentance with the far greater Holy Spirit-baptism of the Christ who was to come. Mark 1:7-8.
3. Jesus, though sinless and thus without need of repentance, nevertheless insisted on being baptized by John (Matthew 3:13-17) for at least two reasons:
   a. Jesus needed to identify Himself with the sinful humanity He came to save. Mark 10:45.
   b. Jesus' burial in and rising out of the water in baptism would dramatize His coming death, burial, and resurrection.

C. Meaning of "baptism"
1. The New Testament word which we translate "baptize" (baptizō in Greek) means, more generally, "dip" or "immerse." It is used twice in the New Testament of Jewish ritual washings. Mark 7:4; Luke 11:38.

2. Most often, however, the New Testament writers use "baptizō" in the special sense of *initiation*. Of course, after Jesus' death, baptism became the Christian sacrament of initiation. To be "baptized into" someone (whether he is Moses, John, or Christ) means to be identified with him and brought under his power and influence. I Corinthians 10:1-2; Mark 1:4-5; Romans 6:3.

II. BLESSINGS ASSOCIATED WITH BAPTISM INTO CHRIST

A. Newness of life through union with Christ in His death and resurrection—"Or do you not know that all of us who have been baptized into Christ Jesus have been baptized into His death? Therefore we have been buried with Him through baptism into death, in order that as Christ was raised from the dead through the glory of the Father, so we too might walk in newness of life." Romans 6:3-4. Baptism "into Christ" represents the Christian's total identification with Christ: so far as God is concerned, the Christian died when Christ died, and rose when Christ rose. What Jesus has done *for* you He wants also to do *in* you. He will not be satisfied with merely changing your life; rather, He wants to give you a new one. II Corinthians 5:17; John 3:3.

B. The "baptism of the Holy Spirit" and derivative blessings
   1. The baptism in, with, or by the Holy Spirit (the Greek preposition "en" can be translated in any of the three ways in English), popularly known as the baptism "of" the Holy Spirit, is *synonymous* with baptism into Christ. Due to the controversy which surrounds the "baptism of the Holy Spirit," this assertion is defended in a separate outline of that title. Here we remark only that by our general definition of "baptism" gleaned from the entire New Testament (see I.C.2.), the baptism in/with/by the Holy Spirit is the initial indwelling of the believer by the Spirit. Moreover, this initial indwelling occurs with the believer's union with Christ at the time of his conversion,

83

since "anyone who does not have the Spirit of Christ does not belong to Him." Romans 8:9.

2. Blessings, and, it should be added, responsibilities which flow from the general blessing of Spirit-baptism include accessibility to the various ministries of the Holy Spirit, including the conviction of sin, the teaching of spiritual truth, and the sovereign giving of one or more grace-gifts ("charismata") to each believer for his use for the benefit of the body of believers. (See the outline, "Fellowship: The Gifts of the Holy Spirit for the Body of Christ.")

3. Some urge that the "baptism of fire" prophesied by John the Baptist is another blessing which comes with the "baptism of the Holy Spirit": "He Himself (Christ) will baptize you in (with/by) the Holy Spirit and fire." Matthew 3:11. They generally equate this aspect of Spirit-baptism with the "tongues as of fire" which on Pentecost rested on each of the 120 believers and led them to speak with other tongues. Acts 2:1-4. However, the immediate context of the rest of John the Baptist's prophecy clearly renders this interpretation impossible: "And His winnowing fork is in His hand, and He will thoroughly clean His threshing-floor; and He will gather His wheat into the barn, *but* He will *burn up* the chaff *with unquenchable fire.*" Matthew 3:12. The baptism of fire is thus a baptism of *judgment* which Christ will administer on the day of judgment (Revelation 20:11-15) to the unrepentant (symbolized by the chaff which will be burned), not to the repentant believer (symbolized by the wheat which will be gathered into the barn). Accordingly, John's words in verse 11 might be paraphrased as follows: "He Himself will baptize *all of you* ('you' here is plural in the Greek)—those of you who truly repent, in/with/by the Holy Spirit when the Christ comes; and the rest of you, with fiery judgment later. Take your pick!"

C. Full-fledged membership in the universal body of believers in Christ—"For by one Spirit we were *all* baptized into one body, whether Jews or Greeks, whether slaves or free, and we were *all* made to drink of one Spirit." I Corinthians 12:13. When we enter into new life with Christ and receive the Holy Spirit as God the Father's promise to us that He *will* complete the work of redeeming us, we are also given a world-wide family of all those who have also entered into this new life with Christ. I Peter 2:9-10. By God's grace we have the privilege of worshipping and fellowshipping with a local body of Christians. But once again this blessing is also a responsibility: when Jesus Christ calls us to Himself, He calls us to each other simultaneously. Notwithstanding Cain's evasive reply to God (Genesis 4:9), we *are* our brother's keeper.

III. CANDIDATES FOR THE SACRAMENT OF WATER-BAPTISM

A. All who confess Christ as Lord are to be baptized in water.

   1. In the Great Commission, our Lord commanded His disciples to baptize converts in the name of the Father, Son, and Holy Spirit as an integral part of their going and teaching "all nations." Matthew 28:19. A complementary command to the convert to be baptized can certainly be inferred from this.

   2. In his Pentecost sermon Peter urged each of his listeners to "be baptized in the name of Jesus Christ." Acts 2:38. A little later "those who had received his word were baptized, . . . about 3000 souls." Acts 2:41. Repentance, in the context of their having heard and received the gospel preached to them, was the sole prerequisite of baptism.

   3. The example of the New Testament church in Acts in consistently baptizing new believers indicates that the other apostles also regarded water-baptism as a divine directive. Acts 8:12-13; 8:36-38; 9:18; 10:46-48; 16:14-15, 33; 18:8; 19:5; 22:16. In each instance the one(s) baptized had heard and received the word of the Lord; only in one

85

case does Luke record a request by the new believer to be baptized. Acts 8:36-38.

B. The purpose of the commandment of the baptismal sacrament in the life of every believer is at least threefold.

  1. Baptism is a *public* testimony by the new believer of the Lordship of Christ in his life ahead. It is the proclamation to all that the blessings associated with baptism into Christ have been secured for the believer.

  2. Baptism is a memorable event in time and space which marks a definite break in the new believer's life and thus can serve as an added encouragement to him in the future to live according to his new, redeemed nature. II Corinthians 5:17; Ephesians 4:1.

  3. Baptism, which should be administered in the presence of the local body of believers which the new Christian has joined or intends to join, serves also to unite the new believer with the others *in fact*, as well as in theory. The event should impress upon them their responsibility to love and care for the new believer, resulting in a net increase in healthy interdependence within the body. Romans 12:10; I Corinthians 12:25.

C. Infant baptism

  1. Arguments in favor

    a. Baptism is for the children of the new covenant in Christ's blood just as circumcision was for the children of the Abrahamic covenant. Colossians 2:11-12.

    b. Paul writes that the children of believing parents are "clean" and "holy," without any qualification as to the faith of the children. I Corinthians 7:14.

    c. Paul and Silas urged the Philippian jailer who sought salvation: "Believe on the Lord Jesus, and you shall be saved, you *and your household.*" Acts 16:31. This command-promise *preceded* Paul and Silas' preaching the gospel to him and his household and the subsequent conversion and baptism of all of them (verses 32-34), suggesting to some that by *his* belief the promise of salvation would include his household.

2. Arguments opposed

   a. Nowhere in the New Testament is infant baptism explicitly commanded or urged.

   b. In all of the baptisms recorded in Acts (see III.A.3.), there is not one example of an infant baptism.

   c. The record of individual baptisms in Acts suggests to some the exclusive rule that baptism should be administered only to those who can give an intelligent profession of faith in the Lord Jesus Christ.

3. Conclusion—It seems best to admit that there is no *direct* Biblical teaching on infant baptism and to recognize that differences in practice among Christians are thus largely differences in preference. However, it should be noted that there is a bigger question lurking just below the surface. Churches that allow or encourage infant baptism tend to emphasize the sovereign election of God, apart from the will of the individual, in salvation; churches that forbid or discourage it tend to stress individual choice and accordingly require that a stage of accountability have been reached. If you are in doubt about infant baptism, consult with your pastor and with his assistance make your decision in the light of God's Word.

4. Rebaptism

   For those who have been baptized as infants and who later come to profess, of their own will, Jesus as Lord, there arises the question of whether or not to be rebaptized. As with infant baptism, the New Testament does not deal directly with this question. Some have urged that Paul's use of the words "one baptism" in Ephesians 4:5 precludes the rebaptism of those baptized as infants. However, the context, which is the five-fold *unity* (hope, Lord, faith, baptism, and God and Father) of the body of believers in Christ, will not support such an interpretation. "One baptism" points to the unifying fact that all

Christians have been baptized in/with/by the *one* Spirit into *one* body. I Corinthians 12:13. The same larger issue of emphasis in salvation is involved here as in infant baptism. Churches emphasizing divine activity in salvation generally prohibit or strongly discourage rebaptism, while churches that stress the human response tend to require or strongly encourage those who were baptized as infants in other churches to be rebaptized. Again, pastoral counselling in a study of Scripture is urged for those in doubt about the matter.

IV. MODE OF BAPTISM

A. Arguments for "immersion"
1. Immersion is in agreement with the etymology of the Greek verb "baptizō," which means "dip" or "immerse."
2. Immersion suits New Testament practice. For example, Philip and the Ethiopian eunuch "went down into the water" and "came up out of the water" in baptism. Acts 8:38-39.
3. Immersion expresses the reality of burial and resurrection with Christ. (See II.A. above.) Romans 6:4.

B. Arguments for "sprinkling"
1. Whatever its etymology, "baptizō" as it is used in the New Testament does not demand immersion. For example, the "baptism of the Holy Spirit" is also described as a "pouring forth." Acts 2:33.
2. The sprinkling of water was required of the Jew in certain situations under Old Testament Law for the purpose of physical and moral purification. Numbers 8:7; 19:17-22. Through the prophet Ezekiel, God promised Israel that He would sprinkle clean water on them and cleanse them from the filthiness of their idolatry. Ezekiel 36:25. And in the New Testament, the author of Hebrews urged his readers to "draw near with a sincere heart in full assurance of faith, having our hearts *sprinkled* clean from an evil conscience and our body washed

with pure water." Hebrews 10:22. Since baptism symbol-izes the same type of moral cleansing involved in these passages, sprinkling is an appropriate mode of baptism.

3. Isolated examples of immersion in Acts cannot be said to imply that immersion is the *required* mode of baptism. It would be no more absurd to insist that every conversion experience parallel Saul's vision on the road to Damascus. Acts 9:1-9. Moreover, the details of Acts 8:38-39, if pressed to mean immersion in every baptism, would also entail the immersion of the *baptizer*.

4. To insist on the symbolism of burial is to ignore other aspects of union with Christ which baptism proclaims, e.g. being "clothed" with Christ. Galatians 3:27.

C. Conclusion—Both immersion and sprinkling are acceptable and meaningful modes of baptism with Scriptural founda-tion. Neither form is commanded in Scripture, either explicitly or implicitly. To recognize the validity of only *one* mode of baptism would thus seem to be making symbolism the issue, rather than the grace of God or the will of the believer. Rather, we should be tolerant of the differing preferences of others in the body of Christ. It is ironic, and tragic, that what God has instituted to symbolize our union with Christ and with the entire body of believers in Him has so often been a source of division within that body.

V. LIMITATIONS OF THE BAPTISMAL SACRAMENT

A. The sacrament of water-baptism does not in itself remove sin; it is rather the inward attitude of repentance and faith which leads to the remission of sin. I Peter 3:18-21. In Romans 10:9-10 Paul mentions only the public confession of Jesus as Lord and the heart-belief that God raised Him from the dead as conditions of salvation, with the former an outgrowth of the latter. Thus, water-baptism is an outward sign of an inner reality. If it were otherwise, we would be saved by *our* work of righteousness, rather than by God's grace (in Christ's death on the cross) through faith, which is the consistent New Testament teaching. Titus 3:5; Romans 3:28; Ephesians 2:8-9.

B. By the same reasoning, the baptismal rite, though commanded by our Lord and by Peter and though carried out faithfully in the New Testament church, must not be presumed to be a *prerequisite* of the forgiveness of sins.

   1. The Apostle Paul's conviction that Christ sent him not "to keep baptizing" but "to keep preaching the gospel" indicates that baptism is not a *necessary* element in preaching the gospel. I Corinthians 1:17. In verses 13-17, while he does not repudiate the importance of baptism, Paul clearly de-emphasizes it in relation to preaching the gospel.

   2. We have an example in Acts 10:44-48 in which Peter's listeners received the Holy Spirit not only before they were baptized in water but moreover, before he finished his message! Surely this is not the usual order, but it helps us to understand a very important truth revealed by a study of Acts: The only systematic statement that we can make about the Holy Spirit is that the Holy Spirit does not work systematically. We may recall Jesus' warning to Nicodemus against prescribing conditions or evidences for the Holy Spirit's coming. John 3:8. It may well be the case that there are many born-again Christians who, for one reason or another, have never received the sacrament of water-baptism.

   3. Two Biblical passages are commonly raised in objection to this.

   a. Jesus' statement to Nicodemus in John 3:5—"Truly, I say to you, unless one is born of water and the Spirit, he cannot enter into the kingdom of God." Some urge that Jesus is laying down *two* prerequisites for entrance into the kingdom of God—water-baptism and spiritual rebirth. However, the context (3:1-12) shows us that Jesus is contending with Nicodemus' ignorance of spiritual things. The emphasis in verse 5 thus belongs on the words "and the Spirit," for Jesus is trying to help Nicodemus see the indispensability *not* of water-baptism but rather of spiritual rebirth, or birth "from above" (verses 3 and 7), for entrance into God's kingdom. Jesus is saying no more, and no less, than that water-baptism, without spiritual rebirth, is not sufficient for entrance into the kingdom of God. The context of His remark does not support the converse assertion that spiritual rebirth without water-baptism is likewise insufficient. Other Christians attempt to escape this problem altogether by suggesting that "born of water" refers not to water-baptism but to physical birth. Admittedly, this does seem to follow from Nicodemus' question in verse 4, but the problem here is finding a clear parallel between water-birth and physical birth. Moreover, the former view is more consistent with the close connection between water-baptism and Spirit-baptism elsewhere in the Gospels. John 1:33; Matthew 3:11.

b. Peter's remarks about baptism in his Pentecost sermon—"Repent, and let each of you be baptized in the name of Jesus Christ for the forgiveness of your sins; and you shall receive the gift of the Holy Spirit." Acts 2:38. Some urge that *both* repentance and baptism in the name of Christ are prerequisites of the forgiveness of sins and the reception of the Holy Spirit. Unfortunately, the precision of the Greek in which the New Testament was originally written is in this instance lost in the English translation. "Repent" is a plural verb and "your" (in "your sins") is also in the plural, but "let each of you be baptized" is in the singular. If the baptismal rite is, as urged, indispensable to the forgiveness of sin and the reception of the Holy Spirit, then Peter's statement would have to mean that each of his listeners needed to be baptized for the forgiveness not only of his own sins, but also of the sins of *everyone else* in the crowd. Clearly, Peter was not intending to say this. Far more reasonable and more in accord with the Greek here is the suggestion that true repentance, in the context of their having heard and received the gospel of Jesus Christ (Acts 2:14-37, especially verse 37), is the sole prerequisite of the forgiveness of sins and the reception of the Holy Spirit; and that the commandment of baptism in the name of Christ, although it is to be obeyed, is nevertheless a *parenthesis* here which does not in itself affect the occurrence of either of the two results of repentance mentioned here, one way or the other.

C. Thus, "to be or not to be" (baptized) is a question which arises only *subsequent* to salvation, and which involves the believer's *obedience* to His Lord and Savior. As a result, in urging another Christian who has never been baptized in water to heed this Biblical commandment, we must never state, explicitly or implicitly, that his *position* in Christ in any way hangs in the balance. From the moment he first trusted in Christ alone for his salvation, his sins have been covered by the blood of Jesus Christ.

8

THE BAPTISM
OF THE HOLY SPIRIT

I. INTRODUCTION

A. The Holy Spirit is the divine agent of unity among *all* believers in Jesus Christ. I Corinthians 12:13. Nevertheless, disagreements concerning the ways that the Holy Spirit works in the lives of believers have tragically often resulted in division. This has particularly been the case with the doctrine and experience of the baptism of the Holy Spirit.

B. Disagreement generally centers around the answers given to one or more of these three questions:

  1. Is the baptism of the Holy Spirit an experience which is distinct from, and *subsequent* to, conversion to Jesus Christ, and which, accordingly, not all Christians have had?

  2. Are there *conditions* which a believer in Christ must meet in order to be baptized with the Holy Spirit?

  3. Is speaking in tongues (i.e. in a language the speaker has never learned) invariably the *initial evidence* of the baptism of the Holy Spirit?

C. Our strategy in seeking the answers to these questions is a careful examination of the relevant portions of the Bible, which is God's inspired Word to us and *the* infallible rule of faith and practice. II Timothy 3:16-17. The answers are not to be found in any one person or group's experience, or lack of experience, for Scripture is the objective standard by which all subjective experience is to be tested for conformity.

D. Our interest in discovering the answers to these questions is not primarily academic, nor is it controversial; rather, it is practical and personal: What is God's perfect will for my life?

E. More specifically, our concern here is not to deny the validity of a claimed experience, but rather to discover the proper Biblical interpretation of that experience, so that we might know whether or not it is an experience which God wants all Christians to have. Much of the division within the body of Christ over this issue has been caused by the failure of Christians of both persuasions to grasp and make clear the distinction between challenging the validity of an alleged experience and accepting the validity of the experience but sincerely questioning the inference drawn from the experience and from Scripture that this experience is available to, and Biblically urged upon, *all* Christians. Doing the former is inherently threatening and likely to be divisive; doing the latter tactfully and in love need not be.

F. Our answers to the three questions in B above are all *no*. The remainder of this outline is devoted to a Biblical explanation and defense of these answers, in turn, including responses to some of the major arguments commonly raised in objection.

II. THE QUESTION OF THE RELATIONSHIP OF THE BAPTISM OF THE HOLY SPIRIT TO CONVERSION

Is the baptism of the Holy Spirit an experience which is distinct from, and subsequent to, conversion to Jesus Christ, and which, accordingly, not all Christians have had?

No, the baptism of the Holy Spirit is an *initial* and a *universal* Christian experience: all born-again believers were baptized with the Holy Spirit at the time of their conversion to Christ.

A. As we noted in the outline on baptism, the word "baptism" was used by the New Testament writers in the special sense of initiation. To be baptized into Christ means to be introduced to Him, to become identified with Him, and to be brought under His power and influence. Similarly, to be baptized in, with, or by the Holy Spirit (the Greek preposition "en" lends equal support to all three translations in English) means to be introduced to the realm of the Holy Spirit and to be brought under His power and influence.

B. Thus, the baptism of the Holy Spirit refers not necessarily to the believer's most powerful experience with the Holy Spirit, but rather to his *first* experience with the Spirit, viz. to the Spirit's taking up permanent residence within the believer. Some Christians have claimed that there are two distinct steps in God's perfect will for the life of a Christian. First, he receives Jesus Christ and is born again (John 3:3) into God's forever family. Then, some time after this he receives the Holy Spirit. However, the testimony of the New Testament is that the reception of the Holy Spirit occurs at the moment of conversion, when the believer is first united with Christ in His death and resurrection.

1. All of God's sons have the Holy Spirit in their hearts. Galatians 4:6. Stated negatively, "if anyone does not have the Spirit of Christ (i.e. the Holy Spirit), he does not belong to Him." Romans 8:9. See also I Corinthians 12:3.

2. Every Christian's body is a temple of the Holy Spirit who is in him. I Corinthians 3:16; 6:19.

3. The Father, Son, and Holy Spirit are *each* actively involved in the salvation of every believer: God the Father "saved us . . . by the washing of regeneration and renewing by the Holy Spirit, whom He poured out upon us richly through Jesus Christ our Savior." Titus 3:5-6.

Thus, the Holy Spirit regenerates us and begins the lifelong process of renewing us from within at the moment of our salvation.

4. In Galatians 3:26, Paul notes that we are sons of God "through faith in Christ Jesus." In Romans 8:14, he asserts that all of God's sons "are being led by the Spirit of God." Thus, in order to be led by the Holy Spirit we need only have faith in Christ.

5. All of God's sons are assured by the Spirit of their sonship and of God's love. Romans 5:5; 8:15-16.

6. Although before Christ's ascension the disciples were told by Him to wait for the Spirit's coming (Acts 1:4), after Pentecost Peter preached that no longer was there any need to wait. "Repent . . . and you shall receive the gift of the Holy Spirit." Acts 2:38. The future tense of the reception of the Spirit extends no further into the future than does the individual's repentance.

7. As one instance in which the baptism of the Holy Spirit did not occur subsequent to conversion, the Gentiles of Cornelius' home in Caesarea received the Holy Spirit while Peter was still preaching, even before they had made any outward response of faith. Acts 10:44.

8. Paul taught that the baptism of the Holy Spirit is the great uniting factor for the body of believers in Jesus Christ, but it would be a dividing factor if it were the case that some Christians have been baptized with the Holy Spirit while others have not. Even to the proud, quarrelsome, and sin-tolerant Corinthian Christians he wrote: "For by one Spirit we were *all* baptized into one body, . . . and we were *all* made to drink of one Spirit." I Corinthians 12:13.

9. None of the authors of the New Testament epistles ever exhorted their readers to receive or be baptized with the Holy Spirit, as we would expect if some Christians had not received this experience. Nor did they urge them to experience any other allegedly new and distinct blessing.

On the contrary, they *assumed* that God gave all of them His Holy Spirit when they received Christ by faith. Romans 5:5; Ephesians 1:3; I Thessalonians 4:8; I John 3:24. 4:13.

C. A variation of the theory that the Holy Spirit is given to the believer subsequent to his conversion is that He is given *partially* at the time of conversion, and fully at a later time, when the believer is baptized with the Spirit. However:

1. This theory is also incompatible with the initiatory meaning of the word "baptism" as used by the New Testament authors. Moreover, some of the same points raised in B above (viz. 6-9) apply against this theory as well.

2. Paul assumed not only that all of his Christian readers had received the Holy Spirit but also that the Holy Spirit had been "poured out upon" all of them "richly through Jesus Christ our Savior." Titus 3:5-6. See also Romans 5:5. Generosity, not partiality, characterizes all of God's giving, including His gift of the Spirit to the believer at conversion. Moreover, this gift, as Christ promised, is not ours temporarily but forever, and is irrevocable. John 14:16; Romans 11:29.

3. Nowhere in Scripture is this theory explicitly taught, nor is there any evidence in Acts of a first and partial entry of the Spirit followed by a second and complete entry. (For a discussion of John 20:22 and Acts 2:1-4, which are most commonly offered as evidence for this view, see D. I. below.)

D. Common objections to the view that all believers are baptized with the Holy Spirit at the time of their conversion to Christ

1. Biblical objections
   a. John 20:22; Acts 2:1-4.
      Objection: The disciples received the Holy Spirit when Jesus breathed on them and told them to receive the Spirit, but were baptized with the Spirit later, on the day of Pentecost.
      Answer: The disciples had no lasting experience

with the Holy Spirit before Pentecost, when they received, i.e. were baptized with, the Holy Spirit in John 20:22 for these reasons:

(1.) Jesus had told them earlier that He had to leave them before the Holy Spirit could come to them: "It is to your advantage that I go away; for if I do not go away, the Helper (i.e. the Holy Spirit) shall not come to you; but if I go, I will send Him to you." John 16:7.

(2.) Only 10 disciples were present at this time: Thomas was not there (John 20:24) and Judas' place was not yet filled. Just as there were 12 tribes of Israel, there needed to be 12 apostles to sit on the 12 thrones judging the 12 tribes. Matthew 19:28. It is unlikely that Christ would have given the Spirit, the agent of unity, to these 10 before the other two could be present.

(3.) In view of Peter's repeated denial of Christ (John 18:15-27), after His resurrection Jesus asked Peter three times if he loved Him. John 21:15-22. This questioning of Peter's allegiance would have made little sense if the Holy Spirit had *already* been given to Peter in John 20:22.

(4.) If the Holy Spirit were in fact given in John 20:22, the Spirit's effect on the disciples was negligible at best, since their old natures, including their continued inability to understand the true nature of Jesus' mission as a spiritual rather than political one (see Acts 1:6), persisted without apparent change until Pentecost. On and after Pentecost, however, there was a great change in the life-style of the disciples. They boldly preached the gospel, performed miracles, freely shared their material possessions, and fellowshipped, prayed, and listened to the apostles' teaching "continually" and "with one mind." Acts 2:40-47. Thus, in light of

Jesus' promise in John 16:7, "Receive the Holy Spirit" (John 20:22) meant "Receive the Holy Spirit *when He comes upon you.*" Jesus' breathing on the disciples was a prophetic act in anticipation of what was to happen on the day of Pentecost. There is a whole string of such acts in the Old Testament, and Jesus' cursing the fig tree in anticipation of the destruction of Jerusalem (Matthew 21:19) is another example of a prophetic act in the New Testament. The early chapters of Acts describe a transitional period in God's plan: the Holy Spirit was given first to Jewish believers in Christ in chapter 2, then to Samaritan believers (half-Jews) in chapter 8, and finally to Gentile believers in chapter 10. Thereafter in Acts, and today, the Holy Spirit is given to the believer as a "down-payment" for his belief (Ephesians 1:13-14) at the moment he receives Christ by faith.

b. Acts 8:14-17.

Objection: These Samaritan believers had previously been "baptized in the name of the Lord Jesus" but had not received the Holy Spirit.

Answer: Here it is clear that those who received the Holy Spirit had been Christians previously as a result of Philip's campaign in Samaria. Acts 8:5-13. However, these were the first Samaritans to come to Christ, and the Jews had had "no dealings with Samaritans" for centuries. John 4:9. If perpetuated, this rivalry might have resulted in a disastrous division between Jewish and Samaritan Christians. Perhaps for this reason God deliberately withheld the gift of the Holy Spirit from the Samaritan believers until the two leading apostles could come to investigate and confirm the genuineness of their conversion. In this way, Peter and John became the needed organic link between the Samaritan and Jewish Christians. This event marks an important transition in Acts; thereafter, half-Jews receive the Holy Spirit when they receive Christ.

c. Acts 19:1-7.

Objection: These disciples had been baptized but had not received the Holy Spirit.

Answer: These 12 men were called "disciples" but were actually disciples of John the Baptist (v. 3). They had never heard of the Holy Spirit (v. 2). Moreover, they had to be told that it was Jesus in whom John had told them to believe (v. 4). It is not surprising, then, that Paul concluded that they were not Christians at all and baptized them "in the name of the Lord Jesus" (v. 5). Their spiritual rebirth and Spirit-baptism thus occurred simultaneously, in verses 5 and 6. Given Paul's subsequent response, his initial question in verse 2 ("Did you receive the Holy Spirit when you believed?") indicates that if a person has not received the Holy Spirit, he has not believed in Christ, as he asserts explicitly in Romans 8:9.

2. *Practical objection*: If all Christians have been baptized with the Holy Spirit, the majority do not appear to have been. Furthermore, some Christians claim that they have received a second, deeper experience of the Holy Spirit, and their life-styles often appear to support that claim. *Answer*:

a. There is no Biblical support for the view that the baptism of the Holy Spirit is always a "spectacular" event. The supernatural signs associated with Pentecost are no more typical of every Spirit-baptism than those on the road to Damascus are of every conversion. Every baptism of the Spirit is a miraculous, supernatural event in God's sight, but from the human perspective many genuine Spirit-baptisms are quite "unsensational."

b. The baptism of the Holy Spirit is the initial, not-to-be-repeated Christian experience. In contrast, the *fullness* of the Holy Spirit is a blessing which flows from the baptism of the Holy Spirit but which must be continuously appropriated to be enjoyed. Paul does not exhort his Christian readers to be baptized with the Spirit, but rather to "keep on being filled" (continuous present imperative) with the Spirit. Ephesians 5:18. The fullness of the Spirit is intended to be the permanent result of the initial experience of Spirit-baptism. Acts 6:3; 7:55; 11:24; 13:52. At the same time, situations often demand a refilling of, or fresh empowering by, the Holy Spirit, particularly when there is a need for the Word of God to be preached with boldness. Acts 4:8, 31; 13:9.

c. Thus, the low spiritual level at which tragically many Christians live today is evidence not of their need to be baptized with the Spirit but rather of their need to recover, by repenting of their unwillingness to let God be the God of their lives and by returning to fellowship with Christ (I John 1:9), the fullness of the Spirit which they have lost because of their sin. Paul makes this point clear in his first letter to the Corinthian Christians: although they had all been baptized with the Spirit (12:13) and the church had been enriched with all of the spiritual gifts (1:4-7), he rebukes them as being "carnal" (3:1), i.e. not Spirit-filled. It is thus possible, and unfortunately common, for Christians (who have been baptized with the Holy Spirit) to cease to be filled with the Spirit because of their unconfessed sin. If you are a Christian, the crucial question is not: "Have you received the baptism of the Holy Spirit?" (the answer is yes), but rather: "Are you *now* filled with the Holy Spirit?"

d. This is sufficient to explain why so many Christians, who have been baptized with the Holy Spirit, do not show it by their life-styles. Needless to say, it does not excuse the carnal Christian for his mediocrity. However, it does help to explain why *some* Christians do

101

indeed have deeper experiences of the Holy Spirit months or even years after their conversions. God's perfect will is a continuous and increasing appropriation of the Spirit, but because of our backsliding into sin, God may use the refilling of the Holy Spirit that follows our repentance and return to fellowship to give us in this sense a new and deeper experience with the Spirit. We may have a hundred such "second" experiences or blessings, but there is no single experience with the Holy Spirit which is the second stage of God's purpose for *all* of us.

E. Thus, the baptism of the Holy Spirit is synonymous with baptism into Christ. There is no need for separate baptisms into each Person of the Trinity. We are baptized *once* "in the name of the Father and the Son and the Holy Spirit." Matthew 28:19.

III. THE QUESTION OF CONDITIONS FOR THE BAPTISM OF THE HOLY SPIRIT

Are there conditions which a believer in Christ must meet in order to be baptized with the Holy Spirit?

No, the baptism of the Holy Spirit, like salvation, is entirely an experience of God's grace. The principal condition for the giving of the Spirit is the work of Jesus Christ, viz. His death, resurrection, and ascension. John 7:37-39; 16:7. Since we have seen that every Christian is baptized with the Holy Spirit at the moment of his conversion to Christ, the only qualification for receiving the Holy Spirit is saving faith in Christ. In particular, the believer does not need to seek after, or ask or pray for, the baptism of the Holy Spirit.

A. There are four metaphors used in the New Testament to describe the baptism of the Holy Spirit. The Holy Spirit is:

1. A garment to be worn—Luke 24:49: "until you *are, clothed* with power." Compare Galatians 3:27; Romans 13:14; Colossians 3:10.

2. A bath—Acts 1:5, "you shall *be baptized* with the Holy Spirit."

102

3. The supernatural source of energy—Acts 1:8, "you shall receive power when the Holy Spirit *has come upon* you."

4. The possessor—Acts 2:4, "they *were all filled* with the Holy Spirit." See also Ephesians 5:18.

Note that in each of the four metaphors, God is the actor and man is the recipient. Our egos would rather fulfill prerequisites for the baptism of the Holy Spirit, but God's gifts are unconditional. I Corinthians 4:7.

B. Jesus consistently referred to the baptism of the Holy Spirit as the *promise* of the Father, not, for example, as the responsibility or the privilege of the believer. Acts 1:4. In Acts 1:5, He said to all of His disciples, "You *shall* be baptized"—not, "You *might* be baptized," "You *can* be baptized if you . . .," or "You *ought* to be baptized." See also John 14:16; 15:26; 16:7-15. Moreover, He gave them no instructions as to what they were to do in preparation; they were merely to wait. Thus, the baptism of the Spirit is a gift, not a challenge, for God's way is grace not law. A gift cannot be earned; it must be received. Galatians 3:2, 5; Romans 5:5; II Corinthians 1:22; 5:5; Ephesians 1:14; I John 3:24; 4:13.

C. Neither at Pentecost nor anywhere else in Acts does any individual or group seek, ask, or pray to be baptized with the Holy Spirit. See, for example, Acts 2:1-4; 4:8, 31; 8:14-17; 9:10-19; 10:44-48; 13:9; 19:1-7. In none of these passages was the Holy Spirit given because those who received Him had asked for Him. It is certainly proper, even desirable, for believers to ask for the Spirit continually (Luke 11:13), but it is not necessary to do so in so many words in order to have the Spirit's presence. In Acts 4:23-31, the disciples prayed for boldness in speaking God's Word, and the result was the filling of the Holy Spirit. Thus, simple prayer appropriates God's continual provision of His Holy Spirit whether the Spirit Himself is specifically requested (Luke 11) or not (Acts 4).

D. None of the authors of the New Testament epistles ever exhorted their readers to ask or pray for, or do anything else in order to receive, the baptism of the Holy Spirit. Instead, as we noted earlier, they *assumed* that God gave them His Spirit when they received Christ by faith. Romans 5:5; I Thessalonians 4:8; I John 3:24; 4:13.

E. Some Christians have claimed that the removal of all known sin is a condition for the grace of the Holy Spirit. However, the Scriptural witness is that the Spirit is the *source* of moral life, not the *goal*. Christ's finished work has released us from the law. Galatians 3:10-14; 4:4-7; Romans 6:14. Accordingly, we "receive the promise of the Spirit through faith." Galatians 3:14. Obedience, then, is not the prerequisite for, but rather the result of, the gift of the Holy Spirit. In Acts 5:32, Peter told the Jewish high priest that another witness of these things is the Holy Spirit, "whom God *gave* (past) to those who *are obeying* (present) Him"; he did not say, "whom God will give to those who obey Him" or "whom God gave to those who obeyed Him." This is not mere semantic quibbling: the very first church council (Acts 15) was called to deal with this very issue of law versus grace (vv. 1, 5). Their conclusions (vv. 23-29) were bathed in grace. The gifts, like the calling, of God are not dependent upon our obedience, but are granted in spite of our disobedience, in order that He alone might be glorified.

F. Luke's inclusion of Simon the magician's attempt to gain the power to bestow the Holy Spirit by bribing the apostles, and of Peter's subsequent rebuke, is his warning to us not to set up conditions for that which is God's free gift, viz. the baptism of the Holy Spirit. Acts 8:18-24.

IV. THE QUESTION OF THE INITIAL EVIDENCE OF THE BAPTISM OF THE HOLY SPIRIT

Is speaking in tongues invariably the initial evidence of the baptism of the Holy Spirit?

No, speaking in tongues may or may not accompany one's baptism with the Holy Spirit. The initial evidence of Spirit-baptism is the same as the initial evidence that the person is a Christian, viz. profession of faith in Jesus Christ. Later, the evidence of a genuine Christian faith and Spirit-baptism is the development in the believer of the fruit of the Holy Spirit.

A. Speaking in tongues is not the invariable sign of the baptism of the Holy Spirit.

    1. Nowhere in Scripture is it explicitly stated that tongues is the initial evidence of Spirit-baptism. On the contrary, in Paul's letter to the Romans, in which Paul gave his most complete statement about our salvation and subsequent life in Christ, tongues are not explicitly mentioned once, even though every other doctrine essential to living in this world as a Christian is carefully treated. Moreover, Paul's list of some of the gifts of the Holy Spirit in Romans 12:6-8 does not mention tongues, although his list in I Corinthians 12 does.

    2. Of all of the groups who received the Holy Spirit in the book of Acts, only three are said to have spoken in tongues. 2:1-4; 10:44-48; 19:1-7. There are no grounds to infer that all of the other people and groups spoke in tongues as well. By the way, those who did speak in tongues did not ask or expect to.

    3. Paul's teaching on the gifts of the Holy Spirit in I Corinthians 12 clearly indicates that tongues is one of a number of gifts, which not all believers are given: "To one is given the word of widsom . . . and . . . to another various kinds of tongues. . . ." The Holy Spirit distributes "to each one individually just as He wills" (vv. 8-11).

    4. Some Christians have accordingly postulated that there is a difference between the tongues in Acts and those in I Corinthians 12-14, the former referring to the *sign* of tongues which, supposedly, all Christians display when they are baptized with the Spirit; and the latter, to the *gift* of tongues which only some receive. However, in I Corinthians 12:30, Paul asks: "All do not speak with

105

tongues, do they?" NO! is the answer contemplated by the Greek formulation. Note that he did not write merely that all do not have the gift of tongues, which would parallel what he had written just before with respect to the gift of healings. Thus, it cannot be argued that all who are baptized with the Holy Spirit display the sign of tongues.

B. Nevertheless, genuine Holy Spirit-inspired speaking in tongues does occur when *some* people receive the Holy Spirit. Some Christians have argued that all of the so-called "sign gifts" (viz. healing, prophecy, miracles, tongues, and interpretation of tongues) ceased as bona fide gifts of the Holy Spirit at about the end of the first century, just after the New Testament was completed. The passage generally cited in support of this is I Corinthians 13:8-12, in which Paul notes: ". . . If there are tongues, they will cease; . . . For we know in part, and we prophesy in part; but when the perfect comes, the partial will be done away . . ." The claim is that the "perfect" is the completed New Testament canon of Scripture, and that the need for authentication of God's message by supernatural signs dissipated after the New Testament was written. However, this seems to be a rather strained interpretation. The passage as a whole suggests that the "perfect" more likely refers to our future condition when Christ returns for us and gives us glorified bodies like His own. I Corinthians 15:50-53; I John 3:2; Romans 8:29. Therefore, I Corinthians 13 does not justify the prohibition of tongues today, in private devotions or in corporate worship. Paul does, however, suggest several prerequisites for the exercise of tongues in a group. An interpreter must be present. I Corinthians 14:28. Speaking in tongues should be limited to two or three people and one at a time; there must not be any chaos. I Corinthians 14:27, 33, 40. Finally, although the immediate effect of the gift of tongues is the edification of the individual (I Corinthians 14:4), the ultimate purpose of this gift, like all of the others, is the edification of the body of believers, which rules out tongues in a situation where it might be divisive or "cause a brother to stumble." I Corinthians 14:26; Romans 14:13. A mature caution is needed here.

C. Inasmuch as the Holy Spirit always has his "finger" pointing to Jesus Christ, reminding us to glorify Christ, not the Spirit (John 15:26; 16:14), the evidence par excellence of the baptism of the Holy Spirit is the glorification of Jesus Christ.

D. If there must be clear and recognizable initial indications of faith, they are adequately satisfied in the prayer "Abba! Father!" (Romans 8:15; Galatians 4:6) or in the confession "Lord Jesus" (I Corinthians 12:3; I John 4:1-3). Both are spoken. If it is objected that this is not sufficiently "supernatural," it must be recognized that generally the demand to see a special evidence of God's presence is not praised in Scripture. Matthew 12:38-42; 16:4; John 7:3-5; 20:29; Romans 8:23-25.

E. As time passes, the evidence that a person has been baptized with the Holy Spirit and is now filled with the Spirit is the formation of a Christ-like character, i.e. the development of the *fruit* of the Holy Spirit (love, joy, peace, patience, kindness, goodness, faithfulness, gentleness, and self-control—Galatians 5:22-23). The mere fact that a person displays some of the *gifts* of the Spirit does not imply that he is now filled with the Spirit, as our earlier discussion on [page 101] of the Corinthian Christians indicates. In the one and only passage in all his letters in which Paul describes the consequences of the fullness of the Spirit (Ephesians 5:18-21), all of the four consequences are moral in nature. "Singing and making melody with your heart to the Lord" and "always giving thanks for all things in the name of our Lord Jesus Christ to God, even the Father" concern our relationship with God; "speaking to one another in psalms and hymns and spiritual songs" and "being subject to one another in the fear of Christ," our relationship with others. The marks of the fullness of the Spirit are thus ultimately seen not in private, mystical experiences but in moral relationships with God and our fellow man. This passage does not imply that continual ecstasy, or "spiritual drunkenness," is the evidence of the fruit of the Spirit, for self-control is part of the fruit of the Spirit (Galatians 5:23) and we are told by Paul not to get drunk with wine precisely because of the loss of self-control involved in doing so.

V. CONCLUDING EXHORTATIONS

A. To those who have received no "spectacular" experiences of the Spirit

1. Do not automatically be suspicious of or deny the validity of such experiences out of pride, envy, or spiritual insecurity. Be careful not to attribute the work of the Holy Spirit to Satan. By all means, "test the spirits" (I John 4:1—see also I Thessalonians 5:21), but if there is nothing in a claimed experience which is contrary to Scripture and the fruit of the experience seems to be edifying to the believer and to the church, then accept it as the work of the Spirit and praise God for it. Do not try to put the Holy Spirit in a box. Perhaps the most systematic statement that we can make about the Holy Spirit is that the Holy Spirit does not work systematically! Failing to see this may result in your quenching the Holy Spirit by trying to contain Him within your own traditional patterns. I Thessalonians 5:19.

2. At the same time, do not allow yourself to fall into sinful dissatisfaction with what appears to the world to be "normal" operations of the Spirit within you. No single spiritual gift is needed for Christian maturity, nor is any one gift evidence of greater spirituality in those who have received it. The test of a believer's spirituality is the development within him of the fruit of the Spirit, not the manifestation of external signs or religious emotion.

B. To those who have received some "spectacular" experience of the Spirit

   1. Worship and praise God for the experience He has chosen to give you, but do not place an unbalanced emphasis upon it. Remember that the foundation for faith is not your subjective *experience*, but is rather the objective *fact* of Christ's life, death, and resurrection. Moreover, do not assume that the Holy Spirit necessarily wants to give *all* Christians the experience He has given you. Paul writes of being caught up into the "third heaven" and hearing "inexpressible words, which a man is not permitted to speak" (II Corinthians 12:2-4), but does not urge this experience upon his readers. The fruit, not any single gift or experience, of the Holy Spirit should characterize all Christians. Accordingly, base your exhortation to others upon the exhortation of Scripture and not upon your own particular experiences.

   2. Specifically, as Scripture does not teach that Spirit-baptism is a second and subsequent experience distinct from conversion which must be actively sought, do not urge Christians to be baptized with the Holy Spirit. Moreover, do not "put an obstacle or a stumbling-block in a brother's way" (Romans 14:13) by claiming contrary to Scripture that speaking in tongues is invariably the sign of the baptism or of the fullness of the Holy Spirit. Instead, urge all Christians to do what *is* urged in the Bible, viz. keep on walking in and being filled with the Holy Spirit. Galatians 5:16; Ephesians 5:18. That is done by presenting our bodies as living and holy sacrifices to God, moment by moment, in obedience to Jesus Christ our Lord. Romans 12:1.

C. To every Christian

   1. Seek continually to be filled with the Spirit, to be led by the Spirit, and to walk in the Spirit. Urge others, in love, to do the same.

   2. Make glorifying Jesus Christ your aim in life, just as it is the Holy Spirit's ministry. John 16:14. Urge others, in love, to do the same.

3. Strive to keep channels of communication open with Christians who hold views on any of these issues which are contrary to your own, but who are also seeking to glorify Jesus Christ. Let us not allow Satan the satisfaction of dividing us on the basis of our doctrines surrounding the very Agent of unity Himself. We are living in a world that is dying without Christ; we have no time to waste quibbling among ourselves.

VI. BIBLIOGRAPHY

A. Bruner, Frederick Dale. *A Theology of the Holy Spirit—The Pentecostal Experience and the New Testament Witness.* William B. Eerdmans Publishing Company, 1970.

B. Stott, John R. W. *The Baptism and Fullness of the Holy Spirit.* Inter-Varsity Press, 1964.

PART TWO

MOVING OUT INTO THE WORLD

9

PERSONAL EVANGELISM: SHARING THE WEALTH

I. BASIC PRINCIPLES OF EVANGELISM

A. The *origin* of evangelism lies not in man but in God, who created man in His own image to be in a vital personal relationship with Him. In spite of our rebellion against His authority, God loves us and considers us worth saving. Genesis 1:26-31; Psalms 8:3-8; Romans 5:6-8.

B. The *foundation* of evangelism is the Great Commission given to the apostles by our Lord Jesus Christ. The essence of that commission is not per se to "win" converts but rather to build disciples, true followers of Christ. Matthew 28:18-20; Mark 16:15; Luke 24:45-49; John 20:21; Acts 1:8.

C. The *agent* of evangelism is the church, i.e., the body of true believers in Jesus Christ. II Corinthians 5:18-20; I Peter 2:9. It has been well said of the church that it is the only society that exists for the benefit of its non-members. True evangelism is not a program per se, nor is it the effort of individual Christians. Rather, it is the natural (or better, *super*natural) outgrowth of the proper functioning of God's community of believers, each of whose life-style (words and deeds both) witnesses to the power of Christ to change lives. Matthew 5:16. Jesus does not entrust this task to a select group of "professional Christians" but to every one of His followers. Christ sent His disciples out into the world two-by-two so that they could support, pray for, and learn from each other. Mark 6:7. We, too, are to come together to go out together. Personal evangelism is not "loner" evangelism.

D. The *motivation* for evangelism is a genuine spiritual life based on our commitment to Jesus Christ, and as a corollary, a loving concern for the nonbeliever who is not experiencing the abundant life God has for all those who love Him. John 10:10; 15:5; I Corinthians 2:9. Without this commitment of oneself to Christ, a vital personal witness is an impossibility. Matthew 12:34.

E. The *power* for evangelism is the Holy Spirit, who is God's gift to all Christians at the time of their spiritual rebirth. Romans 8:9.

   1. The Holy Spirit's relationship to the church in evangelism

      a. The Holy Spirit fills Christians for boldness in witness. Acts 4:31-33; 9:17-20.

      b. The Holy Spirit gives gifts to the church for outreach. Romans 12:1-8; I Corinthians 12-14; Ephesians 4:7-16; I Peter 4:10, 11.

      c. The Holy Spirit chooses some for special outreach, even though we are all to be witnesses to Jesus Christ. The church, however, is to recognize and endorse this choice. Acts 13:1-3.

      d. The Holy Spirit guides believers in outreach. Acts 8:26-40 (Philip and the Ethiopian eunuch); Acts 10 (Peter and Cornelius and the Gentiles in Caesarea); Acts 16:6-10 (Paul and Silas and the Macedonian vision).

   2. The Holy Spirit's relationship to the world (John 16:7-11)

    a. The Holy Spirit convicts men of the grave implications of their sin. John 16:9.

    b. The Holy Spirit convicts men of the certainty of the judgment of their sin. John 16:11

    c. The Holy Spirit convinces men of the truth of the claims of Jesus Christ on their lives. John 15:26.

F. The *key* to all evangelism is love. God calls us to show others the same unconditional, undemanding love God has revealed to us in Christ. John 13:34,35; Romans 5:8; I John 4:19. We cannot ask others to believe that God loves them if we don't love them.

G. Evangelism, then, is building disciples of Jesus Christ. This involves an active concern for the total needs—physical as well as spiritual—of the individual. John 6:5-14; Mark 2:1-12; Matthew 25:31-46; James 2:15-18. Ministering to spiritual needs extends beyond proclaiming the gospel to the unsaved: in addition, new believers must be instructed, individually and collectively, in God's Word on how to live. Accordingly, the next outline suggests some principles of follow-up.

H. There are many ways Christians can and should collectively witness for Christ to the masses of nonbelievers. Evening evangelistic church services, evangelistic Bible studies in homes or dormitories, and campus rallies with an evangelistic speaker are several examples of what can be done. In the remainder of this outline, however, we shall confine ourselves to a consideration of how to "share the wealth" that is ours in Christ with an *individual* non-Christian.

II. INTERNAL BARRIERS TO WITNESSING

A. Paralyzing attitudes

    1. Doubt—We may not really be convinced that Christianity is true. Non-Christians will usually sense our confusion and react negatively to us and to our message.

    2. Fear of rejection by one's non-Christian friends—We may be afraid to stand up for what we believe because we may be ostracized by our non-Christian friends. John 12:42,43. But "perfect love casts out fear." I John 4:18. Moreover, although we must be willing to be ostracized for Jesus' sake, often the reason for our ostracism is that, by our attitudes, we have unwittingly condemned others for their style of life. We must learn to live graciously in a non-Christian world.

3. Pride—Even if we aren't afraid of rejection by our non-Christian friends, we may have deep-seated pride. Often we are more concerned about what the other person will think of us than of Jesus. We need to be willing to be misunderstood for Him.

4. Fear of offending others—Forcing the gospel on an unwilling listener and preaching *at* others as though we are better than they are, are admittedly both fruitless and a bad witness, but withholding the gospel from someone for fear of offending him is evidence of either our lack of genuine concern for his welfare or our disbelief that he is in a desperate condition without Christ. It's a life and death matter—now and eternally. We are thus being irresponsible if we fail to tell him the truth merely because it may be initially unpleasant for him. People don't want to be pushed but do generally appreciate our being honest with them.

5. Insecurity—Our failures as Christians may lead us to keep quiet about the Lord rather than to acknowledge them, claim victory and forgiveness through the blood of Christ, and launch out in faith. I John 1:9. Particularly if we are young, we may be reticent about sharing Christ with others who have had more "experience" in life than we. Satan will always be accusing us that we aren't good enough to talk to anyone about Christ, but we invite others to trust Christ not because we are outstanding Christians but because of who Jesus is. II Corinthians 4:5; Romans 8:1,33,34.

6. Aversion to particular methods—It is true that there are

many approaches, but disagreement with one approach does not justify doing nothing. Quibbling over methods can be a smokescreen for fear. We can use any Biblical method of proclaiming the gospel, but let's do it.

7. Fear of our inability to answer the questions of the non-Christian

   a. We must be willing to admit at times that we do not know the answer and also to offer to dig it out if possible and meet back with the person later.

   b. We must realize that Christianity doesn't crash to the ground in a heap because of our failure to answer one question. Some of the world's greatest minds have tried to disprove it, and Jesus still stands above criticism.

   c. There is, however, no excuse for continued ignorance, and we now turn from problems in attitude to problems in knowledge.

B. Lack of knowledge

1. What our message is—We need a clear understanding of what our message is, and how we can best convey it to a non-Christian. See part III.

2. How to start a conversation on spiritual matters—We need to know how to redirect a conversion away from superficial things to the essential needs of the person and to Jesus Christ as God's provision for these needs. See part IV.

3. Answers to typical questions asked by non-Christians— We should be aware of the questions usually raised by non-Christians and have our basic responses to them thought out in advance. See part V.

III. OUR MESSAGE

A. What it is not

1. Churchianity—A person does not become a Christian by joining a church. This is not meant to imply that we

ought not to attend, support, and join a church. However, it has been said that one can live his entire life in a garage and not be a car. Similarly, a person can spend his entire Sunday-morning (or Wednesday-evening) life in church and yet not be a real Christian.

2. Ethics—Christians should definitely be law-abiding citizens and have high ethical standards, but one can have these attributes and still not be a real Christian.

B. What it is—God became man in the person of Jesus of Nazareth for our:

1. Past—Jesus offers forgiveness of our sin.

   a. Sin is the self-centered refusal to let the God of the universe be the Lord of one's own life. This basic *sin*, of which we are all guilty, manifests itself in many *sins*, involving our actions, omissions, thoughts, and motives. Romans 3:10; Isaiah 53:6.

   b. God's standard for our lives is absolute perfection. Matthew 5:48; Galatians 3:10; James 2:10. As a result of our sin, we have all failed to live up to this standard. Romans 3:23.

   c. God's holiness requires that He judge our failure to live up to His perfect standard, and our sentence will be eternal separation from Him. Romans 1:18; 6:23.

d. However, out of love for us God gave Himself in Christ on the cross in order that we might not have to serve that sentence. Although He was tempted in every way that we are tempted, Jesus lived a perfect life and consequently did not deserve death. Hebrews 4:15. By His death and three-day separation from His Father, Jesus thus served our sentence for us. Romans 5:8; I Peter 2:24; 3:18. He now acts as our Attorney before His Father, pleading our case: "Yes, Father, they are guilty, but forgive them, for I have served their sentence." I John 2:1. Forgiveness of sin is entirely an experience of grace: we can do nothing to earn or deserve it. Ephesians 2:8-9; Titus 3:4-7. See also the outline "Why Jesus *Had* to Die."

2. Future—Jesus offers eternal life.

Christ's resurrection from the grave was necessary:

a. To confirm the fact of the substitutionary nature of His death (i.e. for human sin). I Corinthians 15:17. How else would we know that His death was in any way different from that of anyone else?

b. To conquer the last obstacle to eternal life, death itself. Death is no longer the "NO" over all of human life and accomplishment, for because He lives, we too shall live eternally with Him. John 3:16; 6:40; Romans 6:23.

3. Present—Jesus offers companionship.

Christianity is not just "pie-in-the-sky, by-and-by." Our eternal life begins the day we receive Jesus and thereby enter into a new life of fellowship with God. John 10:10. By His earthly life and death, Jesus identified with our loneliness. By His resurrection, He shattered this loneliness and became our eternal friend. Matthew 28:20.

We must *individually* receive Christ by faith as our personal Lord and Savior to experience the forgiveness of sin, eternal life, and companionship He offers us as a free gift. This is done by praying to Him and asking Him to enter and take

control of our lives. John 1:12; Romans 10:9, Revelation 3:20.

IV. OUR COMMUNICATION OF THIS MESSAGE

Although each situation is different and the use of the same rigid approach with every non-Christian limits the Holy Spirit, there are a number of basic principles that hold true in nearly every situation. We are indebted to Paul Little for these general principles, which are set forth in chapter 2 of *How to Give Away Your Faith*. Our Lord illustrated them in His meeting with the woman at the well. John 4:1-26.

A. We should go where non-Christians are (verses 1-6). Christians are called out of the world in order to be sent into it. John 15:19; 17:15-18. Jesus' conversation with the woman at the well was made possible by the fact that His disciples were not with Him. It is very easy, but wrong, to become a "hop-along Christian," bouncing from Bible study to prayer group all week long so that there is no time left for establishing relationships with non-Christians. We certainly need Christian fellowship, but the proper balance must be sought.

B. We should establish a common interest (verses 7-8). Others will be more likely to ask about our interests once we have talked to them about theirs. Many people are inwardly crying out for someone to listen to them. *LISTEN!!* Not only is listening the key to assessing their needs so that we can perhaps help to meet them, but more importantly, our listening *attentively* is our best way of communicating our (and God's) love for them as individuals. Moreover, discovering that we share an interest with them in athletics, art, literature, or the like can be very helpful as a way of establishing a relationship.

C. We should arouse interest (verses 9-15).

  1. By what we do

    a. The key here to all that follows is the *love* we show the non-Christian by listening to and thereby affirming him, by telling him we care about him, and by proving we care by sacrificing to help him. We must become "second-mile Christians."

    b. Non-Christians are liable to notice and be curious about our calm in the midst of pressure. Acts 16:25-34.

  2. By what we say

    a. We should seek to develop a clear concept of the gospel and of its relationship to the particular interests of others so that we will be able to direct a conversation naturally from a non-Christian's immediate interests to the gospel.

    b. In accordance with our particular situation, we should learn to make remarks designed to elicit questions about spiritual matters from a non-Christian if he is interested. If he's not, we should move on to another subject of conversation, for only the Holy Spirit can create spiritual interest. However, if he does take the initiative by asking a question, all the pressure on us is removed and we can freely share Jesus with him.

    c. Also, we should learn to test for interest by asking questions designed to draw the non-Christian out and direct the conversation toward the gospel without pressuring him. In His earthly ministry our Lord made extensive use of questions in proclaiming and teaching about the kingdom of God. Waldron Scott suggests one possible sequence of questions which has proven useful to some as a springboard to presenting the gospel. These particular questions may be most useful in making "cold contacts," where you had no prior relationship with the person with whom you're talking (e.g. in two-by-two witnessing on the college campus, on the streets, or at the beach or park).

(1.) "Are you interested in spiritual things?" A negative response to this is unlikely, for most people, if properly approached, are eager to discuss spiritual matters with someone who will talk *with*, not *at*, them.

(2.) "Have you ever thought about becoming a real Christian?" An emphasis on "real" may arouse interest in our friend by implying that there may be more to being a Christian than he thinks. If he replies that he doesn't believe in God, we might respond, "Tell me about the god you don't believe in. Perhaps I don't believe in him either."

(3.) "If someone were to ask you, 'What is a real Christian?' how would you answer?" Your wanting to hear his opinion will probably please him. The majority of non-Christians' answers to this question center on the principle of good works, stressing what a Christian *does* rather than what he *is*, viz. a recipient of GRACE, *G*od's *R*iches *A*t *C*hrist's *E*xpense. If our friend's answer falls into this category, we may want to respond, "You know, that's what most people think. I used to think that myself." At this point, human curiosity being what it is, our friend is likely to ask us what we now think a real Christian is.

121

(4.) "Can you spare ten minutes? If you have time, I'd like to show you what the Bible says a Christian is, and how to become one." Even though we have been given the green light to present the gospel, we propose a time limit and ask permission to proceed both to maintain our spirit of courtesy and to assure ourselves of our friend's uncoerced attention. We also indicate that the foundation of our presentation will be the Bible and not our imagination. Moreover, such a question leaves us free to suggest another time and place if our friend says that he does not have ten minutes to spare at the moment.

d. We should be on the alert to seek to identify with problems non-Christians may begin to tell us about as mutual trust develops. They may confess loneliness, lack of purpose, inner emptiness, lack of self-control, frustration, or fear of suffering and death—all of which are symptoms of sin we too have experienced at one time or another. If we empathize with the person by suggesting that we know what it is like and yet add that there is an answer to such fear, anxiety, and boredom, our friend may be receptive to our telling him briefly what we were like, what we're like now, and how we came into a personal relationship with Christ.

e. We should think in advance about ways of responding to particular questions we're asked repeatedly which could lead to a fruitful discussion if handled with care. Here's one example: "Well, hi! What have you been up to lately?" Unthinkingly, we might respond, "Oh, the usual—cramming for exams and playing volleyball occasionally." However, if we'd been preprayered and prepared, we might have answered, "Well, just this afternoon I had the interesting experience of talking to Joe about how Jesus Christ is relevant to life." If the other person displays interest, the conversation is started.

122

f. We may develop a conversation by asking a person what he thinks is wrong with the world. He may ask us for our analysis after he gives us his. If not, we can ask him if he's ever considered what Jesus Christ had to say on the subject and then proceed to point out that His diagnosis was that man's basic problem was and is internal rather than external.

g. We may want to use Christian literature to start a discussion of spiritual matters. We can offer to lend a booklet like "Is Christianity Credible?" or "Becoming a Christian" (Inter-Varsity Press) to our friend with the request that he return it and give us his reaction to it at a later date.

h. Another possible approach is to ask our friend if he knows that many of the specific details of life, death, and resurrection of Jesus were accurately predicted by Hebrew prophets hundreds of years earlier.

D. We should not go too far (verses 16-19). Give the non-Christian no more than he is ready for, or else he may be frightened away by our overeagerness, which betrays insecurity. Picking up a conversation later at the leaving-off point should not be difficult if this principle is followed.

E. We should not condemn (verses 16-19). We should neither condone nor condemn un-Christlike behavior.

1. When we are invited by a non-Christian to do something we'd rather not do, we need to recognize the compliment implicit in his offer and decline on a personal basis in a way that shows him we are not rejecting him. One way to do this is to suggest an alternative activity.

2. We should learn the art of legitimate compliment as a means to create the warmth of feeling essential to an openness to the gospel. Paul began his sermon to the Athenians and his defense before Agrippa (Acts 17:22 and 26:2, 3, respectively) with compliments, and many of his epistles contain compliments soon after the salutation. Romans 1:8; Philippians 1:3ff; Philemon 1ff.

F. We should stick to the main issue (verses 20-26). Jesus did not allow secondary questions to sidetrack Him from the main issue, so neither should we. Of course, we may not get to the point in our first contact with every person, but we should ultimately leave no doubt about the main issue (Jesus Christ).

G. We should confront him directly (verse 26). Our friendship established, sooner or later we should bring the non-Christian into a direct confrontation with the Lord so that he understands his personal responsibility to decide for or against Him. The gospel is much more than a body of facts to be believed: there is the Lord Jesus Christ to be either accepted or rejected. There is no middle ground. Joshua 24:15. But our friendship should not depend upon his response to Christ, and he should be made aware of this. Even if he rejects Christ at this point, we should keep the channels of communication open.

V. DEALING WITH OBJECTIONS TO THIS MESSAGE (APOLOGETICS)

A. Two extremes to avoid

1. Reliance upon human wisdom—We are not commanded to go out into the world to win intellectual arguments but rather to be faithful witnesses in word and deed to Jesus Christ. John 15:27. No answer in itself will bring a person to Christ. Conviction and conversion are the work of the Spirit—not of "persuasive words of wisdom." I Corinthians 2:1-5. A person who is unwilling to believe will not accept anything as evidence.

2. Anti-intellectuality—In light of (1) some claim that we shouldn't try to think out Christianity or answer questions non-Christians ask us, but rather just preach the "simple gospel." But Paul often reasoned with non-Christians. Acts 17:1-3; 18:4,19, etc. Peter exhorts us to be ready to make a defense to anyone who asks us to give an account for the hope that is in us (I Peter 3:15), claiming

elsewhere that faith is based on fact and not "cleverly devised tales" (II Peter 1:16). When God begins to soften hearts, our answers can be used as an instrument to bring others to faith in Christ. "We cannot pander to a man's intellectual arrogance, but we must cater to his intellectual integrity." (John R. W. Stott)

B. Questions commonly asked by non-Christians

Paul Little provides an excellent discussion of each of these in chapter 5 of *How to Give Away Your Faith*, so we shall only list the questions here.

1. "What about the heathen who have never heard of Jesus Christ? Will they be condemned to hell?"
2. "What about the sincere Moslem, Buddhist, etc.? Does he not worship the same God, but under a different name?" In other words, "Is Christ the only way to God?"
3. "Why do the innocent suffer?"
4. "How can miracles be possible? In this scientific age, how can any intelligent person who considers the orderliness of the universe believe in them?"
5. "How do you reconcile faith with the fact that the Bible is full of errors?" More specifically, "Hasn't evolution proven the unreliability of the Bible?"
6. "Isn't it possible to explain Christian experience in purely psychological terms?"
7. "Isn't a good life sufficient to enable a person to enter heaven? If a man has lived a good moral life and done the best he can to qualify for the presence of God, why must he receive Jesus Christ?

Think each of these questions through. What does the Bible say about them? God hasn't given us the complete answer to all of these questions, but we have enough data to show others the intellectual reasonableness of faith in God. With the aid of a Bible dictionary or topical Bible, study up on the ones that stump you. Discuss them with other Christians who are experienced in Bible study and evangelism. Then write out your answers to these questions, for your own benefit and so that you'll be able to give an interested person a copy of your answer to a question which you have discussed together.

C. The case for Christianity summarized

    1. Objective evidence

        a. Historical fulfillment in Jesus Christ of specific Old Testament prophecies concerning the Messiah's first coming

        b. The incomparable life of Jesus of Nazareth

            (1.) His shocking personal claims—for example: "Before Abraham was born, I AM." John 8:58. "I and the Father are one." John 10:30. "I am the way, and the truth, and the life; no one comes to the Father, but through Me." John 14:6. "All things have been handed over to Me by My Father; and no one knows the Son, except the Father; nor does anyone know the Father, except the Son; and anyone to whom the Son wills to reveal Him." Matthew 11:27. Thus, Jesus did not leave us the option of regarding Him as a great moral teacher, yet not God: He must have been a liar, a lunatic, or—as He claimed—the Son of God.

            (2.) His authoritative teaching (e.g. Matthew 5-7) and wisdom in handling opposition (e.g. Mark 12:13-37)

            (3.) His sensitivity to human need (e.g. John 4:5-26; Mark 14:1-9)

            (4.) His miraculous works, illustrating His authority over demons (e.g. Mark 1:21-28), disease (e.g. Mark 1:29-45), nature (e.g. Mark 4:35-41; 6:30-52), and even death itself (John 11:1-44)

            (5.) His bodily resurrection from the dead (Matthew 28; Mark 16; Luke 24; John 20-21)—See J.N.D. Anderson's excellent booklet, "Evidence for the Resurrection," put out by Inter-Varsity Press.

        c. The radically changed lives of many of Jesus' followers after they saw the risen Lord. For example:

(1.) Peter, who had denied Jesus because of a mere servant-girl's questions (John 18:15-18, 25-27, later could not be silenced by the entire Sanhedrin (Acts 4:13-22; 5:27-32).

(2.) Paul, who had overseen the stoning of Stephen and instigated the first great persecution against the church in Jerusalem (Acts 7:58-8:3), met Christ on the road to Damascus (Acts 9:3-9) and later became the leading apostle to the Gentile world.

d. External verification of Biblical events as recorded For example:

(1.) First-century non-Christian writings (Josephus, Jewish rabbis, Tacitus, Suetonius, Pliny, etc.)—See F.F. Bruce, *The New Testament Documents: Are They Reliable?*, William B. Eerdmans, 1959.

(2.) Archaeological discoveries (e.g. the Dead Sea Scrolls)—See William Ramsay, *The Bearing of Recent Discovery on the Trustworthiness of the New Testament*, Baker Book House, 1953.

2. Subjective evidence—*Your* life in Christ, testifying that God is still changing lives in miraculous ways which the world cannot deny

3. Additional bibliography (Inter-Varsity Press)

a. Green, Michael, *Man Alive* and *Runaway World*

b. Lewis, C.S., *Mere Christianity*

c. Little, Paul, *Know Why You Believe*

VI. MISTAKES TO AVOID

A. Don't "water down" the gospel to gain converts. We are distorting the Word of God if, in our witnessing to a non-Christian, we emphasize what Jesus will do for him without also clearly pointing out the necessity of his unconditional submission to Christ's Lordship over his life. Believing facts is not enough: Jesus calls us to follow *Him*.

B. Don't measure success in evangelism in worldly terms, and particularly not in numbers of converts. We must seek to be faithful in our witness to Jesus Christ and leave the results to God. I Corinthians 3:7.

C. Don't allow the pure gospel to be distorted by our culture. In many cases, rejection of our gospel by those in other countries has been a rejection of the United States' way of life more than of Jesus Christ.

D. Don't neglect your spiritual responsibility to be informed of current world and national affairs. As Christians we must live in today's world, and others will tend to write us off if we are consistently uninformed and unconcerned.

E. Don't expect everyone you talk with to become a Christian. There is a characteristic polarization seen throughout the Gospels and Acts. Whenever Jesus or His disciples proclaimed the gospel message, some believed, but others did not. John 11:45-46; Acts 4:1-4; 17:4-5; 28:24.

F. Don't fall into the trap of resigning yourself to merely sowing and watering in evangelism and never reaping. God intends *each* of us to reap. Matthew 9:37, 38. If we fail to see this we become complacent in our witness, and our expecting to fail becomes tragically apparent to the person with whom we are talking.

G. Don't hide your own failure and sin from the non-Christian. The way you handle your failure and sin witnesses to Christ. Acknowledging and confessing them demonstrates to the world the practical remedy for human inadequacy available in the gospel. But if you try to hide failure, you are deceiving yourself, suspending fellowship with God, and probably convincing your non-Christian friend that you're a phony. We are not preaching our perfection but Jesus' perfection. II Corinthians 4:5.

H. Don't neglect to be sensitive to the person with whom you're talking. Learn to listen "between the lines." Pray for a genuine concern and compassion for others that is living proof to them of the reality of Jesus Christ in your life. They will soon detect whether you are doing this because you care or because it's a duty you are reluctantly carrying out.

A heart filled with Christ's love can make many mistakes in sharing Christ and the message will nonetheless get across.

I. Don't neglect to use the Word of God in your witnessing, but on the other hand, continually flipping through the Bible can overwhelm the non-Christian. Memorize key Scripture verses and learn to quote them naturally in presenting the gospel and in responding to questions.

J. In two-by-two "cold contacts" witnessing, don't smother the non-Christian by verbally fighting your partner to "get the message across." In general, one of the two of you should be the leader and do most of the talking, while the other listens attentively and prays silently for his partner and for the other person.

K. Don't allow yourself to stagnate in your witness by failing to learn from your experience. If you are with another Christian when you're witnessing to a non-Christian, ask him for constructive criticism of the way you handled the situation afterwards. When you're asked a question you can't answer, discuss it later with others of wider knowledge so that you'll be prepared for that question the next time it is raised.

L. Don't be impatient for the rebirth of your friends or relatives. Our timetable is often not God's, as Paul realized. Acts 26:28, 29.

M. Don't make the mistake of neglecting to water with prayer the seeds sown in evangelism. On the eve of His death and just after He had given His disciples extensive teaching, Jesus prayed the longest prayer in the Bible. John 17. Paul prayed regularly for his new converts. Philippians 1:3, 4; Colossians 1:9.

VII. BIBLIOGRAPHY

A. Coleman, Robert E. *The Master Plan of Evangelism.* Fleming H. Revell Company, 1963.
B. Kennedy, D. James. *Evangelism Explosion.* Tyndale House, 1970.
C. Little, Paul. *How to Give Away Your Faith.* Inter-Varsity Press, 1962.
D. Packer, J.I. *Evangelism and the Sovereignty of God.* Inter-Varsity Press, 1961.
E. Stott, John R.W. "Personal Evangelism" and "Evangelism: Why and How." Inter-Varsity Press.

10

FOLLOW-UP:
TENDING THE LAMBS

I. WHY WE SHOULD FOLLOW-UP NEW BELIEVERS

A. Just as we are commanded to proclaim the gospel, we are to follow-up those who respond. By "follow-up" we mean disciplining them (Acts 14:21), encouraging them in the faith (Acts 14:22), entrusting God's Word to them (II Timothy 2:2), building them up in Christ (I Corinthians 3:9-15), and watching over and caring for them (I Corinthians 4:15).

  1. Jesus Christ commissioned us to "go therefore and make disciples of all the nations, . . . teaching them to observe all that I commanded you." Matthew 28:19,20. Christ doesn't tell us to make converts but disciples, those who follow Him. True evangelism does not end with the presentation of the gospel. Actually, the real ministry of the Christian only begins with evangelism and continues with follow-up.

  2. After His resurrection Jesus asked Peter three times if he loved Him. John 21:15-17. To Peter's replies of "yes," Jesus told him to "tend my lambs . . . shepherd my sheep . . . tend my sheep." We are to take care of those who belong to Christ, being especially concerned with their spiritual condition.

B. New believers are "babes" in Christ (I Peter 2:2) in that they have certain needs that they cannot fully meet themselves and that we can and should help meet. Some of these basic needs are:

1. Love—The new convert may have heard that God loves him, but he needs to see it acted out before his eyes, so we are to reflect the love of Christ to the new believer. John 15:12. This should be the foundation of any follow-up ministry. Often, this will require some sacrifice and an expenditure of time and money invested in the life of the new believer. I Thessalonians 2:9. This love will grow as we spend time with the new convert and get to know him.

2. Nourishment—The babe in Christ needs to be fed from the Word of God. I Peter 2:2,3. This involves getting him started reading the Bible and directing him to God's Word to answer his questions or problems.

3. Protection—Satan "prowls about like a roaring lion, seeking someone to devour." I Peter 5:8. The new convert is very vulnerable to these attacks. He should be given assurance of his salvation, be taught how to withstand temptation from Satan, and be shown what to do about the sin in his life.

4. Training—Just as parents train their children for the task of living, spiritual parents must also train their spiritual children so that they will be strong and will mature in Christ. This great responsibility involves building upon the foundation that is Jesus Christ with "gold, silver, and precious stones," which are the basic doctrines of the Bible and their application to life. I Corinthians 3:10-15. Well-trained believers are able to share their faith in Christ with others.

C. We need to share and teach others what God has taught us so that *we* will be encouraged and will grow in Christ.

1. Following up a new believer gives us the opportunity to teach others, which we should all be involved in after we have been taught the basics of the Christian life. Hebrews 5:12.

2. The new converts we teach and train will be a source of joy to us as we see how their lives have been changed by the truth God has allowed us to give them. I Thessalonians 2:19-20.

II. GOALS OF FOLLOW-UP

A. The *basic* goal of follow-up is to "present every man complete in Christ." Colossians 1:28. In other words, our concern is to build men and women of God who are mature in Christ, i.e. conformed to His character. Ephesians 4:13; I Thessalonians 2:12; Romans 8:29.

B. The practical aspects of what it means to be mature in Christ serve as *specific* aims in follow-up.

1. The ability to study God's Word and apply it to one's own life is real wisdom and understanding. II Timothy 3:16, 17. This makes a person stable, not "tossed to and fro" by wrong doctrine. Ephesians 4:14.

2. Being faithful and consistent in prayer follows the example of Christ (John 17), Paul (Philippians 1:3, 4), Elijah (James 5:16, 17), and other great men of God.

3. Obedience to God's will produces a maturity in character, morality, and attitudes, and an overall life-style that is Christ-like. John 15:10; Hebrews 5:8; Galatians 5:22, 23.

4. A mature Christian will be *reproductive*: He will bring others to Christ and train them to be mature in Christ. John 17:20, I Thessalonians 1:8.

III. CONTENT OF FOLLOW-UP

A. The New Testament style of follow-up is best described by Paul's reminder to the Thessalonian believers of what he and his team had shared with them: "Having thus a fond affection for you, we were well pleased to impart to you not only the gospel but also our own lives, because you had become very dear to us." I Thessalonians 2:8. In other words, the *basic* content of follow-up is the sharing of our lives in Christ with the new believer.

B. Specifically, however, there are certain basic teachings that we would want to make sure we share with the new believer.

  1. For a brand-new believer (one who has just accepted Christ or who has had no follow-up at all) we would *immediately* want to share with him:

    a. What happened to him when he asked Christ into his life—Explain the whole gospel to him and have him talk about it with you. Relate to him that sins are forgiven not by anything we have done but only through the grace of God exhibited through the work of Jesus Christ on the cross. Ephesians 2:8,9; John 3:14-20; Colossians 1:14. It is because Christ rose up from the grave that we know that this is true. I Corinthians 15:17. When we ask Jesus Christ into our lives, He comes in and we have a new relationship with God as His child. Revelation 3:20, John 1:12. This is the new birth (John 3:3-8), and now we have God's Spirit dwelling in us who makes Jesus real to us, helps us understand the Bible, allows us to experience His peace in our lives, and makes us more like Christ. John 16:7-15; Romans 8:1-17; II Corinthians 3:18.

    b. The ground of his assurance of salvation—The new believer may still not understand all of the gospel nor what his new life really means. In fact, he may doubt that there is any change in his life at all. Explain to him that his salvation is not dependent upon whether he *feels* saved or not. The Christian is to trust God that what He has said in His Word is true. Therefore, show the new convert some of the promises of Scripture. John 6:37; 10:28-29. Also, the Holy Spirit, now resident in the new believer, provides an inner witness

(Romans 8:16), as well as outward fruit (Galatians 5:22, 23), as evidences of a changed life. Other evidences of the Spirit's work include: (1) an increased awareness of sin, (2) a greater hunger for God's Word, (3) a desire for a changed life, (4) an increase in testing, (5) a greater love for other Christians, and (6) a desire to tell others about Christ. Point these out to the new convert as you see them in his life, especially if he is worried about the genuineness of his conversion.

c. How to spend time with God in His Word and in prayer

    (1.) It is very important for all Christians to have a daily devotional time with God in order to allow God to communicate with us. Therefore, explain to the new Christian that he needs this time and that God desires to spend time alone with us. John 4:23. He may need some instruction in how to read the Bible. Urge him to be alert, as he reads, for promises to claim and commands to obey, always seeking to apply what he reads to his own life. James 1:22. If necessary, get the new convert a modern translation of the Bible to read (you may have to buy one for him) and suggest to him a passage to read to get him started. For example, you might ask him to read a chapter of John every day for three weeks.

    (2.) Explain to him that prayer is conversing with God in everyday language. God wants us to share our lives and thoughts with Him. In fact, there are some things that we would want to tell God and no one else. Matthew 6:6. Thanking God for all things (Ephesians 5:20; I Thessalonians 5:17-18) and praying for others (Ephesians 6:18) are two more aspects of prayer we will want to share with the new believer.

    Obviously we cannot share everything we know

concerning Bible study and prayer with the new convert at this early stage in his Christian life. However, we should continue to guide him, answer his questions, and encourage him to share with us what God teaches him from the Word and prayer.

2. As the new believer grows and we spend time with him, we will want to teach him other basics of the Christian life, such as:

a. How to deal with sin in his life—Often the new believer will bring up this subject first because he will be aware of times when he does not allow God to be in control of his life because of an attitude or an act of sin that he knows is displeasing to God. Share I John 1:7—2:2 with him, which tells us what we should do when we sin: confess (agree with God about) our sin and thank Him for His forgiveness and cleansing of our lives. Jesus has already forgiven us of *all* our sin. Explain to the new convert that there will be temptations in his life, but that God has provided a way to meet these temptations. I Corinthians 10:13. God's provision is twofold: the cross of Christ, on which our old sin nature (that part of us that wants to sin) was put to death (Romans 6:6) so that we are no longer bound by it; and the Holy Spirit, who gives us the power to live as God wants us to. Romans 8:13, Galatians 5:16. Read Romans 6—8 with him.

b. The importance of fellowship with other believers

(1.) When we become Christians, we immediately become part of Christ's body, the church. I Peter 2:9; Ephesians 1:22-23. The Bible is clear in its teaching that it is our duty as well as our privilege to meet with our Christian brothers and sisters to worship God, to study His Word, to pray, to celebrate the Lord's supper, and to move out together into a lost world ministering hope and love. Hebrews 10:23-25; Ephesians 4:15,16; Ro-

136

mans 12:4-6; Acts 2:42. God doesn't want isolationist Christians. Just as Ananias introduced Saul of Tarsus to the early church right after his conversion (Acts 9:10-19), we must see that our new brother or sister is welcomed into a Christian fellowship where Christ is preached.

(2.) Once he is involved in a vital Christian fellowship, the new believer may need to be reminded that the others need him no less than he needs them. He is likely to need motivation and guidance in seeking to discover the particular gift(s) the Holy Spirit has given him to exercise for the benefit of the body. He may also need to be encouraged to contribute regularly and sacrificially to the Lord's work through the fellowship of which he has become a part. I Corinthians 16:2; II Corinthians 9:7-8.

c. Witnessing to non-Christians—As the new believer experiences more of his new life in Christ, he will want to share it with others, but he may need some encouragement and direction. If possible, let the new believer be with you some time as you are sharing the gospel with another person, and then provide the opportunity for the new believer to relate what the Lord has done to and for him. As the new convert gains a greater understanding of the gospel he will be more confident to tell others. You may want to share with him how you would lead a person to Christ. He could then even practice presenting the gospel by talking to you as he would to a non-Christian. Encourage the new believer to *write* out his testimony (what his life was like before he became a Christian, how he came to Christ, and how his life has changed since he's become a Christian). Then when he is asked to talk, he will be prepared. I Peter 3:15.

d. The Christian's relationship to the world—The new believer may be concerned about his old habits,

137

friends, and way of life. We are to explain to him that a Christian is to be geographically in the world, yet morally separated from it. II Corinthians 6:17; John 17:14-16. As human beings living in this world we are affected by its value systems and its way of life. However, this world is presently controlled by Satan (II Corinthians 4:4), and we are not to allow ourselves to be drawn away from God by following after the things of the world. Romans 12:2; I John 2:15-17. Often this calls for real heart-searching to determine what is of God and what is of the world. Some questions to put doubtful issues to the test are: "Can I give God the glory while doing this?" I Corinthians 10:31. "Will it cause another Christian to stumble?" Romans 14:21. "Will it give any appearance of evil?" I Thessalonians 5:22. "Will it bring me closer to God?" Philippians 4:8. At the same time, the Christian community is not to isolate itself from non-Christians, for we are to love them and, as part of this love, share God's love in Christ with them. I Corinthians 5:10. In short, we are to be neither "holier-than-thou" nor "worldlier-than-thou."

3. There are many things we will want to share with the new convert that are not listed here. As we continue to spend time with him we will want to introduce him to, for example, the Old Testament, God's future plans (Christ's second coming), the Christian perspective of marriage and vocation, and any other things that have been helpful to us in our Christian life. And as we evaluate his needs, we will want to do everything to "complete what is lacking in (his) faith." I Thessalonians 3:10.

IV. METHODS OF FOLLOW-UP

A. True follow-up is hard work, involving "labor and hardship" (I Thessalonians 2:9) because we are not only sharing a particular teaching, but also our own lives, with the new

138

convert. I Thessalonians 2:8. Follow-up involves a commitment to the Lord to be responsible for the training of a new believer.

B. There are numerous methods of follow-up listed in I Thessalonians, an excellent letter by Paul to study to learn more about follow-up. We may need to use several or all of these methods for each new Christian God has called us to take care of. Some of these methods of follow-up are:

1. Prayer—Prayer is an *essential* element of all follow-up. Since most of the prayers in the New Testament were for new believers, we can use these same requests as we pray for new converts today. Ephesians 1:16-23; 3:14-19; Philippians 1:9-11; I Thessalonians 3:11-13.

2. Correspondence—Most of the epistles of the New Testament were follow-up letters written to encourage and instruct new believers. If we lead someone to the Lord who lives quite a distance from us, or if a new believer moves away from our area, we can still encourage him in his walk with the Lord by writing him about basics that he needs to know, by answering his questions, and by sending him helpful books and pamphlets as he is ready for them.

3. Personal representative—When Paul could not visit a group of new converts, he sent Timothy or another man he had trained to encourage and teach them personally. Philippians 2:19,20; I Thessalonians 3:1,2. Similarly, if the new believer lives too far away from us, we should direct him to a church (i.e. a body of believers) that we know would take personal concern for his spiritual growth. If possible, we should also contact someone in that fellowship and ask him to see that the new believer is welcomed into the body.

4. Personal contact—This is much more effective than 2) or 3) and should be used whenever possible. It involves not only teaching the new convert, but also spending time with him to get to know him better. In this way we can communicate the love of Christ and also our very lives in Christ. I Thessalonians 2:8. One of the best teaching methods is to be an example to the new Christian in everything we wish to communicate to him. I Thessalonians 1:7. For example, since we want him to witness to non-Christians about the Lord, we should take him along with us as we witness.

Our concern for the new convert should be comparable to the way we would take care of a baby—"as a nursing mother tenderly cares for her own children" and "exhorting and encouraging and imploring . . . as a father would his own children." I Thessalonians 2:7, 11. Yet this does not mean that we are to put ourselves above the new convert and act as though we are perfect examples and never sin. Otherwise, the new convert would grow to depend upon us rather than upon God. Be honest about yourself with the new believer and share your shortcomings with him, asking him to pray for you. James 5:16; I Thessalonians 5:25.

C. The *personal* results of our being faithful in applying these methods of follow-up include our own growth in Christ and the joy of seeing others grow in Christ. I Thessalonians 2:19,20. We can even begin to identify with the apostle Paul as he wrote to the believers he had followed up in Thessalonica: "For now we really live, if you stand firm in the Lord. For what thanks can we render to God for you in return for all the joy with which we rejoice before our God on your account?" I Thessalonians 3:8, 9.

V. BIBLIOGRAPHY

A. Moore, Waylon. *New Testament Follow-Up*. William B. Eerdmans Publishing Company, 1963.
B. Booklets for new Christians (Inter-Varsity Press)
   1. Griffiths, Michael. "Encouraging New Christians."
   2. Munger, Robert Boyd. "My Heart—Christ's Home."
   3. Stott, John R.W. "Being a Christian."

11

WHY JESUS *HAD* TO DIE

I. INTRODUCTORY REMARKS

A. The question Why did Jesus *have* to die? is a very relevant one. Paul wrote in I Corinthians 1:23: "We preach Christ crucified, to Jews a stumbling-block, and to Gentiles foolishness." The Jew who fails to distinguish the two Old Testament portraits of the Messiah (Suffering Servant and Conquering King) is still offended by the suggestion of the death of the Messiah. Many others regard the very idea of the death of God's only begotten Son as mere foolishness. We need an answer to the question of why Jesus had to die so that we may be able to understand our own position and to present the gospel clearly and accurately to others.

B. Some have claimed that this question is absurd since circumstances conspired against Jesus to bring about His death. Admittedly, Jesus' claims to being God incarnate offended the Jewish leaders, who had Him crucified by the Romans on a trumped-up charge of insurrection. Nevertheless, the New Testament witness is that His death on the cross was wholly voluntary. Jesus *chose* to die.

1. Far from being taken by surprise, Jesus predicted His death at the hands of the Jews in fulfillment of Old Testament prophecy on numerous occasions during His ministry. Mark 8:31; 9:12; 9:31; John 2:19; 10:11, 15, 18.

2. Jesus' entire life was focused on the day of His death on the cross. He spoke very frequently of His "hour," referring to the crucifixion and to the events directly leading to it. John 2:4; 7:30; 8:20; 12:23; 17:1. Jesus not only predicted His death but also acted it out symbolically before His disciples at the Lord's Supper. Mark 14:22-25; I Corinthians 11:23-26. He told them that the bread represented His body broken for them; the wine, His blood shed for them. The Lord's Supper (the night before the crucifixion) is the divine interpretation of the fact of Jesus' death that is so fundamental to the Christian faith. His death thus represents not the failure but rather the successful completion of His mission on earth. "It is finished!" was His cry of victory as He gave up His spirit. John 19:30. After His resurrection He again explained to His disciples the atoning nature of His death: "Thus it is written, that the Christ should suffer and rise again from the dead the third day; and that repentance for forgiveness of sins should be proclaimed in His name to all the nations—beginning from Jerusalem." Luke 24:46-47.

3. Near the end of His public ministry Jesus claimed that He was laying down His life on His own initiative and that no one was taking it from Him. John 10:17-18. In support of this, Luke wrote that Jesus "resolutely set His face to go to Jerusalem," knowing exactly what lay ahead. Luke 9:51. The events of Christ's last 24 hours provide further support for this claim of His.

   a. For example, instead of attempting to flee from the delegation of Jews and Romans which He knew had

142

been sent to arrest Him, Jesus waited for them at one of His common meeting-places with His disciples. John 18:1-4.

b. Moreover, when Peter drew his sword and cut off the right ear of the high priest's slave (Peter should have stuck to fishing—he usually fared pretty well at that!), Jesus rebuked Him and healed the slave immediately, telling those around Him that He could call down more than twelve legions of angels if He wanted to escape death. Matthew 26:51-54; Luke 22:50-51; John 18:10-11.

c. Before the Jewish high priest and the indecisive and fearful Pontius Pilate, Jesus was decisive and calm. John 18:19-24, 28-40; 19:9-11.

d. Then as final confirmation Jesus' giving up His spirit had several immediate supernatural effects, including the splitting of the temple veil down the middle from top to bottom, an earthquake, the resurrection from the tombs of some of the saints who had died, and the Roman centurion's amazed confession. Matthew 27:51-54.

C. As we shall see, Jesus' death was not only a voluntary act but also an act supremely related to our condition. James Denney pointed out that if you are sitting on the end of a pier and a man runs by, yells "I LOVE YOU!", jumps into the water, and drowns, you will conclude that he was crazy. Why? His love was unrelated to your condition. But if you are in the water drowning and he jumps in, pulls you out, and then says he loves you, you will believe him, for this act was very directly related to your situation.

II. WHY JESUS *HAD* TO DIE

A. Man's Problem—Sin and Its Penalty, Eternal Punishment

1. Man was created in the image of God (Genesis 1:26) for the purpose of glorifying Him. Psalm 86:9; Matthew 5:16; I Corinthians 10:31; I Peter 4:11,16; Revelation

5:13. As created, man was without blemish: "And God saw all that He had made, and behold, it was *very good.*" Genesis 1:31.

2. However, through Adam's disobedience, sin entered into the world. Genesis 3. As a result, man's will was crippled, and all of us have accordingly ratified Adam's original sin by refusing to let the God of the universe be the Lord of our own lives. Even though "through one man [Adam] sin entered into the world, and death through sin," nevertheless "death spread to all men because *all sinned.*" Romans 5:12. "All of us like sheep have gone astray, each of us has turned to his own way." Isaiah 53:6.

3. The result of our having chosen to run our own lives without God is the failure of every one of us to live up to God's perfect and unchangeable standards: "All have sinned and fall short of the glory of God." Romans 3:23.

   a. God revealed these standards to us in the Old Testament Law, principally the Ten Commandments (Exodus 20:3-17), as interpreted and fulfilled by Jesus Christ. In His teachings, particularly the Sermon on the Mount (Matthew 5-7), Jesus repeatedly stressed the point that God's demands touch not only man's *actions*, as the Pharisees had taught, but also his *omissions* (e.g. the parable of the good Samaritan—Luke 10:30-37), *thoughts* (e.g. looking upon a woman to lust for her is equivalent to committing adultery with her in one's heart—Matthew 5:27-28), and *motives* (e.g. Matthew 6:1-18).

   b. Moreover, God's standard is absolute perfection: "You are to be perfect, as your heavenly Father is perfect." Matthew 5:48. Some of us may appear to be faring a little better than others in this endeavor to be perfect, but from God's perspective all that matters is that we are all falling far short. The Law is like a sheet of glass in that once any part of it is broken, the whole pane is shattered: "For whoever keeps the whole law

144

and yet stumbles in *one point*, he has become guilty of all." James 2:10. "Cursed is every one who does not abide by *all* things written in the book of the Law, to perform them." Galatians 3:10. Given this absolute standard, it is not surprising that no man can be justified in God's sight by the works of the Law. Romans 3:20; Galatians 2:16. For as Paul points out, the Law is able to show us what sin is (Romans 3:19-20; 7:7; Galatians 3:19) and to drive us to despair of our own efforts to keep God's commandments (Romans 7:14-24), but the Law cannot impart life to us (Galatians 3:21; Romans 8:1-4) or empower us to obey it.

4. The wages of man's failure to obey God's Law is death. Romans 6:23; Ezekiel 18:4.

   a. First, our sin invariably carries its own punishment to some degree, in broken relationships with others, loneliness, purposelessness, despair, etc. With every sin we commit, we separate ourselves from God and from each other and, like a flower without water, we slowly die.

   b. In addition, our God is a holy God who reacts with righteous anger to our sin. "The wrath of God is revealed from heaven against all ungodliness and unrighteousness of men." Romans 1:18. God is not a wishy-washy galactic grandfather who observes our sin and passes it off with a shrug and a discouraged "Oh, never mind." Throughout the Old Testament God judged and condemned sin. His attitude toward sin is the same today even though He is patiently withholding much of His wrath, "not wishing for any to perish but for all to come to repentance." II Peter 3:9. However, judgment postponed is not judgment avoided, and all of us will one day stand before the judgment-seat of God. Matthew 25; Revelation 20. Since all of us have fallen short of God's perfect standard, we all *deserve* eternal punishment. Try as he

145

will, there is nothing that *man* can do to save himself from this end.

B. God's Problem—The Opposing Dictates of His Love and Holiness

Man's sin is not only man's problem; it is also God's problem. On one hand, just as light and darkness cannot both exist at the same place and time, so also God, by His holy nature, cannot sin or allow sin to be in His presence. Leviticus 11:44-45; Romans 1:18; I Peter 1:14-16; I John 1:6-7. Yet God is at the same time a loving God who takes no delight in the destruction of the sinner. He loves the sinner but hates the sin. The question is whether He can resolve this problem within Himself, and if so, how.

C. God's Solution—The Death of Christ

1. God's solution to man's problem and to His own problem is the death of Jesus Christ.

   a. The death of Christ is the complete solution to God's problem in that God gave Himself in Christ on the cross in order to fulfill the demand of His justice that sin be punished by death. Romans 6:23; Hebrews 9:22. Since Jesus lived an unblemished life of perfect obedience to His Father, including keeping the Law as it had been given by God to Israel, He did not deserve death. John 5:19; 8:46; II Corinthians 5:21; Hebrews 4:14-15; 9:14. Accordingly, when He died voluntarily, He died not for His own sins but for ours, the just for the unjust, in order to fulfill the requirement of the Law (Romans 8:3-4) and thereby to maintain *both* the love and the holiness of God. Romans 5:8; I Peter 2:21-24; 3:18. Christ is our unblemished Passover Lamb who was sacrificed once for our sins for all time. Exodus 12:1-28; Leviticus 17:14; I Corinthians 5:7; Hebrews 9:11-15, 22.

   b. The death of Christ is the solution to man's problem in that it reversed the work of Adam and reestablished man's relationship with God. Since Jesus has already

146

paid the penalty for our sins, we who have received Him as our Lord and Savior will not be judged by God regarding our salvation. John 3:18; 5:24. The requirement of the Law has been satisfied, once and for all. Romans 8:3-4; I John 1:7. Accordingly, instead of seeing us in our sin, God the Father sees Christ and His righteousness in us: God made Jesus "who knew no sin to be sin on our behalf, that we might become the righteousness of God in Him." II Corinthians 5:21. Christ's forgiveness extends to *all* of our transgressions—past, present, and future—for Christ nailed them all to the cross. Colossians 2:13-14. "There is therefore *now no* condemnation for those who are in Christ Jesus." Romans 8:1. By God's grace, and in spite of our sinfulness, we are given the right to become adopted sons of God, and we are "new creatures." John 1:12; Romans 8:14-17; II Corinthians 5:17. We pass out of death and into abundant life, now and forever. John 5:24; 10:10.

2. Some have charged that a benevolent God would not pour out His wrath over our sin on an "innocent third party." However, Jesus, though innocent, is not a third party. He was fully man and is also fully God: Paul wrote that in Him "all the fulness of Deity dwells in bodily form." Colossians 2:9. See also John 1:1; Philippians 2:5-8. "Now all these things are from God, who reconciled us to Himself through Christ, and gave us the ministry of reconciliation, namely, that *God was in Christ* reconciling the world to Himself, not counting their trespasses against them." II Corinthians 5:18-19. In fact, redemption is the work of all three Persons of the Trinity, from start to finish: God the Father "saved us . . . by the washing of regeneration and renewing by the Holy Spirit, whom He poured out upon us richly through Jesus Christ our Savior." Titus 3:5-6.

D. Summary—Jesus *had* to die in order to reestablish the

relationship between man and God which was severed by man's sin. By Christ's death God judges sin and saves the sinner. In this way, God solves both His problem, viz. the opposing dictates of His love and holiness, and our problem, viz. the wages of our sin. Christ's death accomplishes its purpose in us when we are reconciled to our Creator by receiving Christ by faith as our personal Lord and Savior.

III. MISTAKES TO AVOID

A. Do not pervert the meaning of Jesus' death on the cross for our sins by using it as an excuse to continue to live in sin. Galatians 5:13.

    1. As Christ has made us new creatures in Him (II Corinthians 5:17), why would we *want* to return to our former condition of being hopelessly entangled in sin? Sin is now more unnatural for us than is obedience to God. Before receiving Christ we were free to sin; now we are free *not* to sin: "It ain't gonna *reign* any more!" Paul expounds upon this vital truth in detail in Romans 6, his thesis being that we have been freed from the *penalty* of sin, we are in the process of being freed from the *power* of sin, and we will one day be freed from the *presence* of sin. "Even so consider yourselves to be dead to sin, but alive to God in Christ Jesus." Romans 6:11.

    2. Moreover, God's Word contains some very strong warnings to anyone who is tempted to continue sinning willfully after receiving Christ. For example: "If we go on sinning willfully after receiving the knowledge of the truth, there no longer remains a sacrifice for sins, but a certain terrifying expectation of judgment, and the fury of a fire which will consume the adversaries." Hebrews 10:26-27. See also II Peter 2:20-21. These warnings raise the issue of eternal security, or "Once saved, always saved?," to which we now turn.

        a. The references above and others seem to suggest that a person can become a born-again believer in Jesus

Christ and then later lose his salvation. For example: "The one who *endures* to the end, it is he who shall be saved." Matthew 24:13. See also II Timothy 2:12. God the Father "has now reconciled you in His fleshly body through death . . . *if* indeed you continue in the faith . . ." Colossians 1:22-23. See also Hebrews 3:14. "In the case of those who have once been enlightened and have tasted of the heavenly gift and have been made partakers of the Holy Spirit, and have tasted the good word of God and the powers of the age to come, and then have fallen away, it is impossible to renew them again to repentance, since they again crucify to themselves the Son of God, and put Him to open shame." Hebrews 6:4-6.

b. However, other references in Scripture seem to indicate that once a person is saved, he can never lose that salvation. The Lord "does not forsake His godly ones: they are *preserved forever*." Psalm 37:28. Jesus said: "My sheep hear My voice, and I know them, . . . and they shall never perish, and no one shall snatch them out of My hand. My Father, who has given them to Me, is greater than all; and no one is able to snatch them out of the Father's hand." John 10:27-29. See also John 6:37-40. In Romans 8:31-39, Paul asserts that *nothing* "shall be able to separate us from the love of God, which is in Christ Jesus our Lord." Later in the same letter he adds: "The gifts and the calling of God are *irrevocable*." Romans 11:29. See also I Corinthians 1:8; II Corinthians 1:22; Ephesians 4:30; Philippians 1:6. Peter writes: "[God the Father] has caused us to be born again to a living hope through the resurrection of Jesus Christ from the dead, to obtain an inheritance which is *imperishable* and undefiled and will not fade away, *reserved* in heaven for you, who are protected by the power of God through faith for a salvation ready to be revealed in the last time." I Peter 1:3-5. Finally, how can we who did nothing to *earn* our salvation (Ephesians 2:8-9) do anything to *keep* it?

c. Perhaps the best way of reconciling these two seemingly conflicting strands of Scriptural references is by seeing the "perseverance" verses (see [a] above) as true from *man's* perspective and the "eternal security" verses [b] as true from God's perspective. God, who knows the hearts of men perfectly, will preserve those who are His own to the end. However, we finite humans must look upon outward appearances since we cannot know the inward spiritual state of others. I Samuel 16:7. Sometimes these outward appearances will deceive us, and a person who professed faith in Christ, and whom we *thought* was among God's elect, will later renounce Him. We emphasize, parenthetically, that his renunciation entails a conscious, prolonged desire to be totally rid of Christ, not merely a temporary lackadaisical attitude toward one's commitment to Him. From God's perspective, then, it is not *really* possible to lose one's salvation, but from man's finite perspective it is *apparently* possible. Thus, the purpose of the warnings in the "perseverance" verses is not to instill fear in Christians who are seeking to know and carry out God's will for their lives, but rather to bring to repentance Christians who aren't, lest they turn out not to have been Christians at all.

d. Accordingly, we must "persevere to the end" not to keep from losing our salvation, but rather to demonstrate to ourselves and to others that our profession of faith was, and is, genuine. II Peter 1:10-11. In examining ourselves to be certain that we are "in the faith" (II Corinthians 13:5), we must remember that our assurance comes not from our own good works (Isaiah 64:6), but from God, by His Holy Spirit's bearing witness with our spirit that we are indeed children and heirs of God. Romans 8:16-17.

e. In sum, even though this side of heaven our lives will never be free of all sin (I John 1:8-10), one who *willfully* and persistently continues in sin may be demonstrating that his apparent profession of faith was not a genuine conversion and that he never really was saved. Nevertheless, we have no right to judge who has and who has not genuinely received Christ. If a person professes faith in Christ as his Lord and Savior, as the Bible teaches, then we must accept him as our brother in Christ. And if such a person later falls away from the Lord, we should exhort him to repent but we have no right to pronounce final judgment upon him, for he may later return to Christ and thereby prove that he was among God's children all along. God, and only God, knows men's hearts perfectly.

B. Do not let the emphasis of this outline obscure the important fact that Jesus not only *had to die*, but He also *had to rise again* from the grave.

   1. Jesus' resurrection was necessary to confirm the truth of His words concerning the substitutionary nature of His death (i.e. for our sins). I Corinthians 15:17.

   2. Jesus' resurrection was necessary to conquer the last obstacle to eternal life, death itself. Only because He lives shall we too live. John 3:16; 6:40; Romans 6:23.

12

THE CHRISTIAN
AND
THE STATE

I. BASIC PRINCIPLES

A. As Christians, our attitude toward the world should be one neither of total affirmation nor of total denial.

  1. "Our citizenship is in heaven" (Philippians 3:20), but this anticipation of the end of the age upon the return of our Lord Jesus Christ should not lead us to be indifferent to the world in which we now live. Since our Lord took this world seriously by dying for it, we must also *identify with the world in its need.*

  2. At the same time, however, we must *separate ourselves from the world in its sin.* We must not allow ourselves to be contaminated by its false value systems. James 1:27.

  3. In short, we must be in, but not of, the world. John 17:15-18. We must be neither "holier-than-thou" nor "worldlier-than-thou." If we fail to separate ourselves from the world in its sin, we shall have no message; if we fail to identify with the world in its need, we shall have no audience. We must do both to effectively communicate the gospel to the world.

B. As we shall see, this dualism carries over into the Biblical conception of the state as something provisional, to be neither renounced as a matter of principle nor accepted uncritically as something final.

II. JESUS' ATTITUDE TOWARD THE STATE

A. The historical situation

1. The Jewish nation had lost its independence and was under the rule of the Roman state. Although it possessed a certain autonomy within the framework of the Roman state, the Jewish theocratic ideal (the religious community's coinciding with the state) was only realized to a small degree.

2. There were two opposing Jewish positions regarding the Roman state.

   a. The Sadducees gave their unreserved submission to the Roman domination and surrendered all hope of the kingdom of God; they were the collaborationists of the day.

   b. The Zealots (the extreme wing of the Pharisees) unreservedly denounced the Roman state and for years preached and prepared for a holy war. Their efforts led finally to open war, which ended with the destruction of the temple in Jerusalem by the Romans in A.D. 70.

B. Jesus was not a Sadducee

1. Some of His statements do not indicate any particular respect for the Roman rulers. Luke 13:32.

2. He accepted the common Jewish classification of the hated tax-collectors as "collaborationists" and even named them in the same breath with sinners, prostitutes, and the heathen. Matthew 18:17; 21:31.

C. Jesus was not a Zealot

153

1. He openly received the tax-collectors, who were the greatest enemies of the Zealots.
   a. He dined at Zaccheus' house. Luke 19:1-10.
   b. Not only were there Zealots among His disciples (certainly Simon the Zealot, probably Judas Iscariot and Simon Peter, and perhaps also the sons of Zebedee, James and John), but also a tax-collector (Matthew). Matthew 10:2-4.
2. Jesus regarded the Zealotist political understanding of the Messiah as Satanic, for the Zealots confused the kingdom of God with an earthly form of the state aimed at world domination. Mark 8:31-33; John 18:36.
3. The taxpaying incident (Mark 12:13-17) illustrates our Lord's renunciation of both Zealotism and Sadduceeism. The Sadducees advocated paying the required poll-tax to Caesar; the Zealots did not. In His answer Jesus showed that we all have responsibility in two different spheres of existence—human government and divine government. Within its sphere the state can demand what belongs to it, such as money and taxes, but we are to give God—not the state—what is His, i.e. our lives, our entire persons. Cf. John 19:11.

D. Consequences of Jesus' teaching and life
   1. First, Jesus did not regard the state as a final institution to be equated with the kingdom of God. The state belongs to the present age and will definitely vanish when the kingdom of God comes.
   2. However, as long as this age still continues, the state's existence is willed by God—even the existence of the heathen Roman state, although it is by no means of divine nature. Consequently, Jesus' disciple is not to try to abolish the state as an institution but is to give it what it needs for its existence.
   3. As soon as the state demands more than is necessary to its existence, i.e. as soon as it demands what is God's (thus transgressing its limits), the disciple is relieved of all

154

obligation to this requirement of the totalitarian state. In fact, he is not allowed to give to a state what is God's. But even in this case he will not deny the state those things, like taxes, which are necessary to the existence of any state, nor will he proceed against the state by force of arms in the name of the gospel. Waging war may be a matter for the state, but not for the community of the disciples.

III. PAUL'S ATTITUDE TOWARD THE STATE
A. Romans 13:1-7

Paul urged each of his readers to subject himself willingly to the governing authorities, for two reasons: all such authorities are established by God (13:1), so that one who resists them is resisting God and will incur condemnation from Him (13:2); *and* resistance invites the wrath of the authorities, and properly so, for in bringing vengeance upon evil-doers they are *ministers* of God to us for good (13:3-6). The Christian's responsibilities include paying taxes and giving rulers the honor they deserve. On the basis of this passage alone, some classify Paul as a totally uncritical servant of any state, no matter how totalitarian. However, as always, to properly interpret Scripture we must consider the context of the passage. By reading from Romans 12:9 through the end of chapter 13, we learn two crucial things.

1. The matter under discussion in 12:9–13:10 is the Christian commandment of love. The section begins with the exhortation "Let love be without hypocrisy," and ends with the statement "Love does no wrong to a neighbor; love therefore is the fulfillment of the law." The state properly does exactly the opposite of what the Christian is to do: it takes vengeance on evil-doers (13:4), but the Christian is by no means to repay evil with evil (12:17,19). The important truth Paul was proclaiming in 13:1-7 is that Christians are not to oppose the state merely because of this difference.

2. The expectation of the end of the present age is also under discussion (13:12) and reminds us that the state is a temporary institution, which will pass away, but which is nevertheless willed by God for the duration of this age.

B. I Corinthians 6:1-8

Paul's opinion of the state is also under discussion here, where he tells the Christians in Corinth not to submit their controversies to the state for settlement. He is not denying the state the right to administer its own judicial affairs, but he is indicating that there are limits on the state's authority for the Christian: wherever Christians can dispense with the state without threatening its existence, they should do so. In particular, Christians should settle their quarrels without using the state's institutions of justice.

C. Read together, Romans 13 and I Corinthians 6. These two passages indicate that the state is not by nature a divine form to be equated with the kingdom of God, but it is nevertheless willed by God as a temporary, provisional institution to be obeyed as long as it remains within its bounds. For if it were of divine nature, then Christians would be allowed to bring their litigation before the state as well as before the congregation. We thus find in Paul's teachings precisely the same relative attitude toward the state that we saw in our Lord's.

IV. OTHER BIBLICAL PASSAGES

A. Daniel 1-6

Daniel and his trio of friends knew not to obey a human authority to the extent of disobeying God. Note that their resistance was nonviolent and that they were prepared to accept the king's punishment for their disobedience. Daniel 1:8-16; 3:13-18, 28-30; 6:6-23.

B. I Peter 2:11-17

This is a passage quite similar to Romans 13 which is also often taken out of context and isolated from other relevant passages of Scripture. As Peter wrote this letter, we mention several of his statements in Acts which, together with this portion of his letter, illustrate his conception of the state.

1. Acts 4:19, 20—"Whether it is right in the sight of God to give heed to you rather than to God, you be the judge, for we cannot stop speaking what we have seen and heard."

2. Acts 5:29—"We must obey God rather than men."

The apostles' resistance, however, was *nonviolent*: they did not resist arrest in these incidents or later, when many of them were imprisoned and martyred for their faith.

C. Revelation 13

The crucial point to be made here is that, unlike the type of state described in Romans 13 and I Peter 2, the state here depicted as the "beast from the abyss" has transgressed its divinely appointed bounds and has become a totalitarian power, demanding not merely the obedience of its citizens, but their total allegiance, including their worship. Since the state has usurped prerogatives which belong to God alone, the Christian is no longer obligated to, and indeed cannot, obey. Revelation 14:9-11.

V. INFLUENCE OF THE BODY OF CHRIST IN A DEMOCRACY

A. The New Testament church was to a very great degree separate from the totalitarian Roman state. However, "a democratic state places the matter of responsibility in a different light. Here the citizens of local communities and of the nation are the responsible parties for the selection of those who rule over them and therefore ultimately for the laws which the legislative bodies pass. Therefore, I as an individual citizen share a real measure of responsibility for the nature of my government and the laws under which justice is executed. For this reason, the Christian citizen who accepts Romans 13 as a divine revelation for the character of the state must assume a particular sense of responsibility for the character of the state of which he is a citizen." (George Ladd, "The Christian and the State," *His,* 1967)

B. The relationship between the Christian church and the state in a democracy should be one of independence marked by neither a maximum degree of separation nor by domination by either the church or the state. The state's primary concern is the realization of order and justice; the church is to proclaim truth and exhibit love.

C. Since the Lord's church is always to identify with the world in its need, it must be the front line for all who suffer injustice. Christians must speak out loudly and immediately in exposing evil and injustice in society, particularly when the government itself is the instigator of the injustice.

D. There are, however, limits to the proper influence of the church upon the state, for the church must not seek to rule the state. Concern for the rights of man, irrespective of what might happen to the institutional church, is proper influence, but concern only for the church and its worldly welfare as an institution is not. The endorsement of political parties or candidates by the institutional church and the use by the church of the state's coercive power to achieve its own purposes fall into this latter category of unacceptable practices.

E. Perhaps the most important type of impact of the body of Christ on society is *indirect*.

    1. There is and should be a long-term influence by the church on the morals and value systems of the community.

    2. The church's effort to maintain its freedom to proclaim the gospel has helped to keep the door open for the freedom of mankind in general.

    3. Christian social education (i.e. teaching about the meaning of the Christian faith for the great public issues of the day) affects public decisions through the work of individual Christians in their various occupations, their influence on public opinion, and in their political activities as citizens.

F. Every Christian has an individual responsibility to use his influence, voice, and vote to promote justice.

1. We must all carefully evaluate political candidates and parties. There are two major errors to be avoided:
   a. Do not evaluate candidates or parties in terms of a single issue at the cost of neglecting all other important issues of domestic and foreign policy.
   b. Do not let the personal character or piety of candidates determine your vote without taking into account the forces which support them or the wisdom of their policies. The personal character of our leaders is important, but the primary emphasis should be placed on integrity in the discharge of public responsibilities.

2. We must face current issues squarely, taking "every thought captive to the obedience of Christ." II Corinthians 10:5.

3. Some Christians are in addition called to enter the fields of politics and law.

VI. CONCLUSIONS

A. Nature of the state
   1. Human government as such is instituted by God for the duration of the present age (until the return of Christ). Its authority is consequently derivative, delegated, temporary, and limited.
   2. The essential purpose of the state is the maintenance of law and order and the dispensation of justice to mankind.
   3. The state is an order of preservation and not of creation, for if man had not fallen from grace government would be unneccessary.

B. Obligations of the Christian church to the state
   1. The church must loyally give the state everything necessary to its existence.
      a. Christians must pay all required taxes. Matthew 17:24-27; Mark 12:13-17; Romans 13:6-7.
      b. Christians must oppose all anarchy and Zealotism within their ranks.

    c. Christians must obey the state as long as it is functioning in accordance with its divinely established purpose.

2. The church must act as the "conscience" of the state by remaining, in principle, critical toward any state and being ready to warn it against transgression of its legitimate limits.

3. As God alone is Lord of conscience, if the state transgresses its limits and commands the Christian to violate God's commandments, the Christian can and must refuse to obey. However, the Christian must, even in this case, resist nonviolently and must be prepared to accept the punishment the state metes out for his disobedience.

C. There is today, in some quarters, an increasing tendency in our country to write off the government as evil. However, the Christian's attitude toward the government, regardless of his opinions about the wisdom of its policies or the integrity of its officials, should be fundamentally *positive* in that the state's existence in this age is willed by God for specific purposes. In fact, it is precisely the Christian who is able to ascribe a higher dignity to the state—even the non-Christian state—than the non-Christian citizen can do. In exhorting us to pray for our rulers (I Timothy 2:1-4), Paul did not leave us the option either of *destructively* criticizing the government or of being totally indifferent toward it.

VII. BIBLIOGRAPHY

Cullmann, Oscar. *The State in the New Testament*. Charles Scribner's Sons, 1956.

13

RESISTING
THE DEVIL

I. INTRODUCTORY REMARKS

A. The Bible teaches clearly and unequivocally that the devil, or Satan, is both *real* and *personal*.

   1. Jesus' life

   a. Immediately after our Lord's baptism and divine affirmation (Matthew 3:13-17), He was led by the Holy Spirit into the wilderness, where He fasted for 40 days and nights and was then personally tempted by the devil. Matthew 4:1-11. In the context the clear intention of the author is that this passage should be taken literally. Consequently, anyone who has problems believing in a real and personal devil also has problems believing in a real and personal Lord and Savior, for Jesus answered all three of his verbal enticements.

b. When Jesus told His disciples that He had to undergo rejection by the Jewish leaders, be killed, and rise again, Peter took Him aside and rebuked Him. Jesus turned around and addressed not Peter but Satan, commanding him to get behind Him and thereby indicating His belief in a personal devil who works on and in people. Mark 8:31-33.

2. Peter's testimony—After Pentecost, when Peter discovered Ananias and Sapphira's lie, he asked Ananias why Satan had filled his heart to lie to the Holy Spirit and to keep back some of the revenue from the sale of the land. Acts 5:3.

3. Paul's testimony—If there were no enemy, Paul would not urge us to "put on the full *armor* of God, that you may be able to stand firm against the schemes of the devil" Ephesians 6:11.

4. James' testimony—James exhorts us in one breath to submit to God *and* resist the devil, who *will* flee from us when we do resist him. James 4:7.

B. The Bible's clear teaching on the reality and personality of Satan is accompanied by its frequent urging that we actively and diligently resist him. We are told by Jesus to "keep watching and praying" so that we might not fall into temptation (Matthew 26:41), by Paul to "stand firm against the schemes of the devil" (Ephesians 6:11), by James to "resist" him (James 4:7), and by Peter to "be of sober spirit and on the alert" for him (I Peter 5:8,9).

C. These exhortations to resist the devil constitute an indispensable part of our submission to God. "Submit therefore to God" is immediately succeeded by "Resist the devil and he will flee from you." James 4:7. Obviously there are both positive and negative aspects of our submission to God, and this is precisely because when Christ came into the world, He did so to accomplish the salvation of those whom the Father had given Him (positive) and simultaneously to "destroy the works of the devil" (negative). I Timothy 1:15;

162

Hebrews 2:14; I John 3:8. Christ's bodily resurrection sealed Satan's doom, but even though the victory is fully assured (Revelation 20:10), the spiritual war Paul describes in Ephesians 6:11-17 is not yet over. Our baptism into Christ by the Holy Spirit has placed us on Jesus' front line where, as defectives from Satan's ranks, we are subject to his attempts to wound us. Satan knows he's lost us for *eternity*, but not for *time*. As a condemned murderer who's still on the loose, he's dangerous. John 8:44. He lives only to wound Christ but can do so only by hurting His body of believers on earth. Praise God that "greater is He who is in you [the Holy Spirit] than he who is in the world [Satan]." I John 4:4. Inasmuch as Satan will take advantage of us if we are ignorant of his schemes (II Corinthians 2:11), we now turn to a biographical sketch of the devil.

II. SATAN—A BIOGRAPHICAL SKETCH

A. A created being—Satan was created by the Lord Jesus. Colossians 1:16. Created in God's own image, he was wise, beautiful, absolutely perfect in every way, and free to exercise his will. He was second in command to God Himself.

B. His sin—Pride and self-deception energized Satan's desire to be number one, which, coupled with his God-given freedom, led to the birth of sin, as Satan exalted himself against God and took some fallen angels, or demons, with him. Isaiah 14:12-15.

C. The devil fallen—This rebellion brought Satan eternal banishment from heaven, and hell was created for him and his angels. Luke 10:18; II Peter 2:4; Jude 6. But instead of sending them directly, the sovereign God who "causes all things to work together for good" (Romans 8:28) chose to exploit sin by developing a race of tested men and women. His greatness perverted by an unquenchable thirst for self-gratification, Satan still has his wisdom and power and is quite qualified to tempt man.

163

D. God of this world—Satan became the god of this world when the first man, Adam, who had been placed on the earth and told by God to subdue it and to exercise dominion over everything that moved, disobeyed and joined Satan's rebel gang. Sin and death consequently spread to all men (Romans 5:12-21), but all of us have nevertheless ratified Adam's choice by our sins and hence have joined the devil's rebel gang, too. Romans 3:23. However, Satan's defeat at the hand of One mightier than he (Jesus Christ) was announced soon after Adam's fall. Genesis 3:15.

E. His big mistake—Engineering Christ's death was Satan's biggest mistake, for it gave man the very ingenious escape hatch out of the devil's kingdom and into God's. Moreover, Jesus' subsequent resurrection proved the harmlessness of physical death and sealed the devil's fate: his future is everlasting fire. Matthew 25:41; Revelation 20:10. The only question remaining is how many people he will be able to drag down with him. Revelation 20:15. Though a defeated enemy, Satan is still a powerful enemy and continues to tempt man. Acts 5:3; 13:10; I Corinthians 7:5. In fact, he is the *only* source of temptation: God may *test* us but never *tempts* us. James 1:13.

F. His limitations

    1. Not omniscient—If Satan possessed all knowledge, he "would not have crucified the Lord of Glory." I Corinthians 2:8. Nor does Satan know the day or hour of Christ's return. Matthew 24:36.

    2. Not omnipresent—Although Satan does have access to all people, his blows against our bodies appear to be limited to the power of suggestion and the resulting psychosomatic disorders.

    3. Not omnipotent—He obviously cannot take lives at will, or all Christians ("the salt of the earth"—Matthew 5:13) would be dead. Nevertheless, he seems to have great power over the elements, for destruction and death are written everywhere in the universe. However, all of his power is *derivative*. For example, Satan needs God's permission to tempt us. Job 1:12; 2:6; Luke 22:31. Moreover, Satan's power is inferior to the Lord's. I John 4:4; John 14:30.

4. Believer's old nature—Satan has contact with the Christian only through the old nature. He has no access to the new nature received at salvation. Colossians 3:9, 10; II Corinthians 5:17. Since the Christian is always free to choose between his two natures, Satan cannot touch the *will* of the believer. His influence is limited to the subtle intellectual and emotional pressures he can (and does!) exert via the old nature.

G. His advantages—Although the devil is not omniscient, omnipresent, or omnipotent, he does have some important advantages over us for which he must always be *respected*, but never *worshipped*.

1. Centuries of experience in tempting man.
2. Instantaneous and immediate access to our minds.
3. A complete view of our thoughts, including our motives, plans, and ambitions.
4. An awareness of all our strengths and weaknesses, especially our vulnerable spots.
5. Where permitted by carelessness or ignorance, the ability to plant ideas in, or remove ideas from, our minds. John 13:2; Mark 4:15; I Chronicles 21:1.
6. Where given permission by an individual, the ability to possess him in both mind and body. John 13:27.

H. His descriptive names in Scripture
1. A beast. Revelation 19:19.
2. A deceiver. II Corinthians 11:3.
3. A hinderer. I Thessalonians 2:18.
4. A murderer from the beginning. John 8:44.
5. A roaring lion. I Peter 5:8.
6. An angel of light. II Corinthians 11:14.
7. *Our* adversary. I Peter 5:8.

8. Prince of the power of the air. Ephesians 2:2.

9. The father of lies. John 8:44.

10. The god of this world. II Corinthians 4:4.

11. The tempter. Matthew 4:3; I Thessalonians 3:5.

III. THE WAR IN OUR MINDS

A. The mind is the key to the will. We are what we think: as a man "thinks within himself, so he is." Proverbs 23:7. Fully aware that he needs only to capture our thoughts to control us, Satan carries on continuous warfare in our minds. Romans 7:22, 23. The same subtlety which deceived Eve is still present today, and the devil often manipulates our minds with surprising ease. II Corinthians 11:3.

B. As it is the undisciplined mind that is most vulnerable to satanic attack, it is godly discipline in our thought-life which is our basic protection. If we do not consciously control *every* thought entering our heads (and who does?), Satan will be able to introduce his own lies. We must therefore seek to make God's Word—our weapon in this war, the sword of the Spirit—a grid over our hearts which filters out satanic suggestions before they penetrate our minds and appear later in our actions. Ephesians 6:17; Psalm 119:11. We must take "every thought captive to the obedience of Christ" before allowing it to take up residence in our minds. II Corinthians 10:5. Moreover, we must keep seeking and setting our minds on the things above, where Christ is, so that we will not give the devil an opportunity. Colossians 3:1,2; Ephesians 4:27.

C. Satan's basic strategy in seeking to control us is planting and watering the thought in our minds that *he does not exist*.

1. For if he can convince us that he is no more real than Santa Claus (and we must acknowledge that even among Christians he's done a remarkably good job thus far), we will not be alert to his tricks and hence will provide only weak opposition at best.

2. Moreover, he fears an open confrontation with Christ,

166

recalling that he batted 0-for-3 last time (Matthew 4:1-11) and knowing what will happen on the final day of ultimate confrontation.

D. Consequently, Satan has developed a perfect disguise—SELF. There is nothing more subtle than satanic suggestions which arrive in our minds as our own ideas. The devil operates through our natural desires (e.g. success, happiness, etc.) and our own thoughts to enslave us. James 1:14. A person thus does not have to be an open *Satan-worshipper* to be under Satan's control—he can be a *self-worshipper*! The extent to which we live for ourselves is the extent to which we are filled with the spirit of Satan. Mark 8:31-37, especially v. 33.

E. For insight into some of Satan's subtle techniques of temptation, read C.S. Lewis' classic *The Screwtape Letters*, which is a fictional collection of short letters of advice from one demon to another. We mention three tidbits here from chapter XIV for motivational purposes.

  1. If Christ has made us humble, Satan will try to make us proud about it!

  2. Satan will try to get us to think of humility, not as self-forgetfulness as we ought, but as a low opinion of our own talents, spiritual gifts, and character so as to keep us from greater achievement.

  3. Satan will try to get us to make "confident resolutions" and "lavish promises of perpetual virtue" in order to keep us from relying on Christ for the strength to meet the daily and hourly temptations.

IV. RESISTING THE DEVIL

A. Preparation—Put on the full armor of God

No soldier goes into battle unprotected and unarmed. As soldiers in active service to the Lord (II Timothy 2:4), we need to put on the full armor of God if we are to stand firm against the schemes of the devil. Ephesians 6:11. This armor consists of the helmet of salvation, the breastplate of

YOU NEED THE FULL ARMOR OF GOD. EPH. 6:14-17

righteousness, the shield of faith, the sword of the Spirit, loins girded with truth, and the preparation of the gospel of peace. Ephesians 6:14-17.

B. Sharing insight—"Speak of the devil!"

Satan needs darkness to operate effectively, so turn on the light. Acts 26:18. Share with other Christians the knowledge you have acquired about Satan and his tricks. There are many things he will not do with people watching him, so it is important for you to encourage others in your fellowship to be on the lookout, too. Be discerning in your approach, however, if the devil has in the past been largely ignored by them. Start by dropping his name now and then, mentioning perhaps how he can plant ideas in our minds. This does much for your own alertness to his tricks, too.

C. Detection—Watch your weaknesses

Satan's attacks come at our weakest points, so you need to discover:

1. What *your* worst faults are—C.S. Lovett offers this list of some common frailties (based in part on Galatians 5:19-

168

21) in *Dealing with the Devil*: lust, idolatry (allowing *anything* to come between you and the Lord), laziness, touchiness, judgmentalism (e.g. measuring others by yourself), factiousness, gossip, worry, pessimism, doubt, selfishness, distraction, lying (including getting carried away with the facts when telling stories), dissatisfaction, discouragement, wastefulness (of money, time, or talents), abusiveness, covetousness, depression, fear, and procrastination. The natural thing to do is to blame ourselves for these faults. Blaming Satan seems like a cop-out, and he counts on this to protect his disguise.

2. What God's Word has to say about these faults—For example, if procrastination is one of your weakest points, then read, meditate upon, and *memorize* Ephesians 5:15,16: "Be careful how you walk, not as unwise men, but as wise, *making the most* of your time, because the days are evil." Colossians 4:5 ("Conduct yourselves with wisdom toward outsiders, making the most of the opportunity") may also prove helpful. This is a specific application of our general exhortation above to allow God's Word to become a grid over our hearts to sift out unprofitable thoughts. A topical Bible or Bible dictionary is extremely useful in searching for relevant Scripture passages.

D. Shock treatment—Speak *to* the devil!
Jesus spoke to him when He was being tempted, so why shouldn't we also? Matthew 4:1-11. In refusing Satan's offer of power and glory in verse 10, Jesus said, "Begone, Satan! For it is written, 'You shall worship the Lord your God, and serve Him only.' " Verse 11 records His success, "Then the devil left Him." Whenever we discover Satan attacking us, Lovett recommends using the following formula: "Satan! In the name of Jesus Christ, go away! For it is written, . . . (appropriate Bible quote)." The exact wording we use is of course unimportant, but several things ought to be included in our shock treatment for Satan.

169

1. Satan's name—Having caught him in the act of tempting you, you want to shock him by calling him by his name.
2. Jesus' name—"Whatever you do in word or deed, do *all* in the name of the Lord Jesus." Colossians 3:17. Resisting the devil is no exception. Using Jesus' name accomplishes at least two things.
   a. It reminds *us* that our own name is hopelessly ineffective in this spiritual battle, thereby making us conscious of our total dependence on Jesus.
   b. It also startles *Satan*, for he now sees—not us in our fear—but rather the One who defeated him on the cross.
3. Orders to Satan to leave immediately—Having startled Satan with the authority of Christ, you are now in a position to rid yourself of him.

E. Weapon—Use God's Word against the devil
   Addressing Satan by name and ordering him to leave by the authority of Christ is important but is by nature *defensive* and consequently needs to be followed by an *offensive* attack. God's Word to us, described in Ephesians 6:17 as the sword of the Spirit, is the *only* means we have of effectively countering Satan's word to us. Memorizing key

brief passages of Scripture (viz. those which relate to our particular weaknesses) is thus essential not only to help us develop a protective grid over our hearts but also to enable us to defeat the devil at the *moment* of temptation. Here are examples of verses from God's Word dealing with some of the common frailties listed earlier:

1. Lust—Leviticus 11:45; II Timothy 2:22.
2. Idolatry—Exodus 20:3; Deuteronomy 6:13; Matthew 6:24.
3. Touchiness—James 1:19, 20; I Corinthians 13:5.
4. Judgmentalism—James 4:11; Romans 14:13.
5. Factiousness—Romans 14:19; Ephesians 4:4-6.
6. Gossip—Galatians 6:2; James 4:11.
7. Worry—Philippians 4:6; Matthew 6:25.
8. Selfishness—Romans 12:10; 14:7, 8.
9. Lying—Ephesians 4:25; John 8:32.
10. Dissatisfaction—I Timothy 6:8; I Thessalonians 5:18.
11. Discouragement—John 16:33; I John 5:5.
12. Abusiveness—Colossians 3:8; Ephesians 4:29.
13. Covetousness—Colossians 3:2; Philippians 4:19; Psalm 37:4.
14. Fear—John 14:27; II Timothy 1:7.
15. Procrastination—Ephesians 5:15, 16; Colossians 4:5.

V. MISTAKES TO AVOID

A. Don't let your initial doubts about the propriety of talking to the devil keep you from doing so *immediately* upon realizing that he is seeking to invade your mind with a question or suggestion. Remember that his biggest trick is to try to get us to think that he doesn't exist! But a very important part of submitting to God is resisting the devil. James 4:7.

B. Don't think that because you have successfully resisted the devil once or twice (or even many times), he will not return again to work on you. Luke 4:13. We will not be totally rid of Satan until we die or the Lord comes again to take us to be with Him. Our status with respect to sin is that we have been freed from the *penalty* of sin, are in the process of being freed from the *power* of sin, and will one day be freed from the *presence* of sin.

C. Don't become overly Satan-conscious, to the extreme of not also being conscious of the Lord's continual presence within you and of His victory over the devil. This would amount to the inadvertent worship of the devil himself. Remember that "greater is He who is in you than he who is in the world." I John 4:4.

D. Don't carelessly toss around half-truths about the devil. Be discerning in your speech about him in the presence of those who might possibly be caused to stumble. II Timothy 2:15.

E. Don't ever let Satan fool you into thinking that Jesus never experienced a particular temptation that you are facing, and that He thus cannot help you resist it. "For we do not have a high priest who cannot sympathize with our weaknesses, but one who has been tempted in *all things* as we are, yet without sin. Let us therefore draw near with confidence to the throne of grace, that we may receive mercy and may find grace to help in time of need." Hebrews 4:15-16. Notice also that undergoing temptation is not in itself a sin: God is concerned about our *response* to temptation. We close with perhaps the most comforting verse in all of Scripture on the subject of temptation: "No temptation has overtaken you but such as is common to man; and *God is faithful*, who will not allow you to be tempted beyond what you are able; but with the temptation will provide the way of escape also, that you may be able to endure it." I Corinthians 10:13.

VI. BIBLIOGRAPHY

A. Lewis, C.S. *The Screwtape Letters*. MacMillan Company. 1961.

B. Lovett, C.S. *Dealing with the Devil*. Personal Christianity. 1967.

14

DISCERNMENT

I. THE NEED FOR DISCERNMENT IN THE CHURCH TODAY

A. The Bible warns us that within the church there will be false prophets and teachers who will try to lead Christians astray with doctrine that is contrary to God's Word. II Peter 2:1-3; I Timothy 4:1-3. Jesus Christ taught that within the visible church there would be professing believers who are not true Christians. Matthew 7:15-23. Furthermore, an increasing number of false prophets is a sign of the nearness of the end of the present age. Matthew 24:11.

B. In order not to be led away from the true faith by false teaching, the Christian must be able to discern, i.e. distinguish between, what is of God (truth) and what is a deception wrought by Satan (error). Malachi 3:18. Paul exhorts us to "examine *everything* carefully; hold fast to that which is good; and abstain from every form of evil." I Thessalonians 5:21,22; Ephesians 6:11-17.

C. Today especially there are many different kinds of teaching that are claiming divine truth. In order not to remain a spiritual infant "tossed here and there by waves, and carried about by every wind of doctrine, by the trickery of men, by craftiness in deceitful scheming," the believer needs the right equipment, part of which is the knowledge of what discernment is and of its Biblical basis, to which we now turn. Ephesians 4:11-16.

II. GOD'S PROVISIONS FOR THE NEED FOR DISCERNMENT

The Lord has equipped His church with the ability to discern between good and evil and between truth and error. This ability is manifested in several ways.

A. Once we have trusted in Christ for our salvation and have asked Him to take control of our lives, we have God's Holy Spirit dwelling inside of us. Romans 8:9. Paul says that "we have the mind of Christ." I Corinthians 2:16. Because of this, we are able to understand and "appraise" spiritual things, such as the Bible. I Corinthians 2:12-15. Therefore, *every* true believer has *some* measure of spiritual discernment.

B. Our spiritual discernment, which is closely related to wisdom, increases as we become more mature in the faith and "grow up into Christ." Ephesians 4:14,15. This maturity is based not so much on years as on the amount of time spent studying God's Word and putting into practice what is learned. "Solid food [the Word of God] is for the mature, who because of practice have their senses trained to discern good and evil." Hebrews 5:14. This is one important reason why new believers should seek the counsel of church elders and older Christians, especially in matters that require discernment.

C. Among the many gifts that Christ gives to His church (see the outline "Fellowship: The Gifts of the Holy Spirit for the Body of Christ") is the gift of the discernment of spirits. I

174

Corinthians 12:10. This means that there are some members of the body of Christ who have a *special* ability (which must also be properly developed) to distinguish between God's truth and Satan's deception. Since Satan's schemes are very deceiving, a local body of believers can be easily led astray unless this gift is exercised. Clearly, the gift of discernment has as its purpose providing protection for the church.

III. SCRIPTURAL TESTS FOR DISCERNMENT

The basis of all spiritual discernment is not our own *subjective* feelings but rather the *objective* Word of God, and specifically, what God has set up as tests to determine what is of God and what is not. We are instructed not to "believe every spirit, but [rather to] test the spirits to see whether they are from God." I John 4:1. We offer nine Biblical tests for discernment below. The greater the number of these tests that we determine an individual or group fails, the more certain we can be that Satan is involved in the goings-on.

A. Does the doctrine conform to God's Word?

Perhaps the best test to determine whether or not an individual or group is of God is to compare what they teach with Scripture. God never violates His Word. If a scriptural doctrine is violated or ignored, then we must accept God's Word on the matter. II Timothy 3:16, 17. Of course, in this age there will always be differing interpretations of certain passages of the Bible. This makes it all the more vital for us to be faithful and diligent students of *all* of His Word as we ask God for wisdom in discerning the true interpretations of it. II Timothy 2:15; James 1:5.

Criteria B-F below are particularly important doctrinal questions.

B. Is Jesus recognized as having come to earth as a man?

I John 4:2. Those who do not believe in the complete humanity of Jesus have severely distorted the gospel accounts. John 1:14. Paul also teaches very clearly about Christ's humanity in Philippians 2:5-8. The Word of God classifies those who deny this as deceivers. II John 7.

C. Is Jesus Christ recognized as God?
I John 4:14-15. In Matthew 11:27 Jesus makes this astonishing claim: "*All things* have been handed over to Me by My Father; and no one knows the Son, except the Father; nor does anyone know the Father, *except the Son,* and anyone to whom the Son wills to reveal Him." See John 8:58 and 10:30 for several other astonishing claims. Paul clearly teaches both the full humanity and the full divinity of Jesus in one verse: "For in Him [Christ] all the fulness of Deity dwells in bodily form." Colossians 2:9.

D. Is Jesus recognized as the Christ, or Messiah?
Anyone who denies this is a liar and an antichrist. I John 2:22, 23; Mark 14:61, 62; John 4:25, 26.

E. Is Jesus Christ recognized as Lord?
If God's Spirit is truly resident in a person, he will also be able to acknowledge Jesus Christ as *the* Lord of his life. I Corinthians 12:3. For even the demons have an intellectual belief in God and shudder at His power. James 2:19; Mark 8:34.

F. Are the major doctrines of Scripture in the proper perspective?
Myths, endless genealogies, and fruitless discussion over minor scriptural points are evidences of straying from the truth of God's Word. I Timothy 1:3-6; Titus 3:9. Also included in this category are those who add on to the Bible their own scriptures and their own laws that they teach must be followed for salvation. Jude tells us to "contend earnestly

for the faith which was *once for all* delivered to the saints."
Jude 3. Jude wrote this between A.D. 80 and 90, when all of
the apostles except John had died or passed out of the
picture, and was thus claiming that beyond the teaching of
the apostles, no further revelation was to be expected. The
salvation God offers to us is a free gift, purchased with the
blood of Jesus Christ, which we receive through faith in
Him. This redemption is the major theme throughout all of
the Bible. Ephesians 2:8,9; John 3:16; Genesis 15:6.
We now leave the more objective doctrinal tests and turn to
several somewhat more subjective tests concerning behavior.

G. Is God's grace prompting a more godly life-style?
If God's grace, i.e. His unmerited gifts to us of salvation and
of freedom from an external set of rules, is used as an excuse
to continue to walk in sin, then this constitutes a serious
misuse of God's grace and a denial of Jesus as Lord and
Master. Jude 3, 4. See also Romans 6, especially verses 1, 2,
11-14. Of course, none of us is able to carry out the perfect
will of God at all times. Romans 3:23; Isaiah 53:6. However, no one can say that he knows God if he *consistently*
violates and ignores God's commandments for living, the
essence of which is loving God and loving one another. I
John 2:3-6; 3:7-10.

H. Is the fruit of the Holy Spirit in evidence?
Jesus tells us that we will know who the false teachers are by
the quality of their lives. Matthew 7:15-20. The fruit of the
Holy Spirit includes love, joy, peace, patience, kindness,
goodness, faithfulness, gentleness, and self-control, while
the evidence of being controlled by Satan includes immorality, impurity, sensuality, idolatry, sorcery, enmities, strife,
jealousy, outbursts of anger, disputes, dissensions, factions,
envyings, drunkenness, and carousings. Galatians 5:19-23.

I. Are things generally being done decently and in order?

Since "God is not a God of confusion but of peace," anarchy and division are always Satan's doing. I Corinthians 14:33. Because of our own preferences regarding forms of worship, this test is only a *relative* indicator of whether Satan or God is in control and should consequently be used in conjunction with some of the other tests before any decision is made.

IV. OUR RESPONSE

Our response to individuals or groups that we feel are *not* of God is an extremely important—though often neglected—part of our submission to Him. We offer some guidelines below.

A. Do not be quick to pass judgment on or to condemn others.

1. Since we are not omniscient as God is, we cannot fully discern the hearts of men. As humans we are prone to error and can easily misinterpret words and/or actions.

2. We must remember that God is the only true and just Judge. James 4:11, 12. *He* will right the wrongs and bring vengeance upon those who deserve it at the proper time. Romans 12:19.

3. Moreover, we will be judged by God in the manner in which we judge others. Matthew 7:1-5; Romans 2:1-4. The Bible teaches that Christians will not face a judgment for *salvation*, for Christ has saved us from that. John 3:18; 5:24; Colossians 2:13,14. However, every Christian will face a judgment for *rewards* based upon his works. James 2:12,13; Romans 14:10-12; II Corinthians 5:9,10; I Corinthians 3:10-15.

B. With regard to individuals or groups who have erred from the truth, whether due to ignorance or to deception by Satan, we are not to judge in the sense of passing sentence upon and condemning them, but we are instructed in the Bible to judge in the sense of examining, testing, and appraising their *beliefs* and *actions*. James 5:19,20. This is a crucial distinction: we are to judge actions but never

178

motives. I Corinthians 4:5. This correction must be done in a spirit of gentleness and love, without any feeling of superiority. Galatians 6:1-5. If the occasion warrants it (and definitely, for example, if the erring individual is a member of a local church), the instruction and warning should first be done in private, and then in the presence of other believers if the private exhortation is rejected. Matthew 18:15-17. In your exhortation use the Word of God: it's profitable for teaching, for *reproof*, for *correction*, and for training in righteousness. II Timothy 3:16.

C. With regard to those whom we have observed and believe to be not of God, and who reject the truth of God's Word presented clearly, accurately, and uncondemningly to them, the Bible is clear about what our response should be.

1. We are to *avoid* men who teach and proclaim doctrine that is contrary to God's Word. Romans 16:17; II John 10, 11. This separation will protect us from being deceived and may also cause those who are apostate, i.e. those who have fallen away from the truth, to repent and return to the truth.

2. We are not to listen to and get "carried away by varied and strange teachings." Hebrews 13:9. It is dangerous to absorb the teachings of cults and others that are clearly opposed to the truth of God's Word. This also means that we are not to argue with these people. II Timothy 2:14; Titus 3:9. Too many people have followed this route, have had seeds of doubt planted in them by Satan, and have been deceived themselves into accepting the error. As Christ said, we are like "sheep in the midst of wolves; therefore be shrewd as serpents, and innocent as doves." Matthew 10:16.

3. If we are aware of false teaching that is being spread, we are to warn others, *especially new believers* who may not yet have as clear a knowledge of God's Word as we, so that they can discern the truth. Acts 20:29-31.

D. On the positive side, we are to stand firm in the truth. I

Thessalonians 5:21. We can do this by immersing ourselves in God's Word to us and by allowing Him to build us up in the faith by our obedience. Jude 17-21. The whole book of Jude, incidentally, deals with apostasy—the evil of it, the certain judgment of it, and our response to it. This is important because error and apostasy can slip in almost unnoticed, and unless we know what God's Word says and are living it and proclaiming it, we may also be deceived. Jude 3, 4.

E. The presence and danger of apostasy should cause us to be alert and strong in our faith—*not fearful.* God's Spirit in us is greater than Satan, the deceiver of this world. I John 4:4. Christ's promise to us as Christians is that no person or thing can ever separate us from Him and His love. Romans 8:35-39; John 10:27-29. We can be confident that Christ will continue to work in us until the day of His return in glory, when we will be presented blameless and complete before God the Father. Philippians 1:6, 9-11.

15

THE CHRISTIAN
AND ILLEGAL DRUGS

I. BASIC PRINCIPLES

A. The question of a Christian's using illegal drugs (i.e. all drugs not available in a drug store with or without prescription, including marijuana, heroin, LSD, etc.) is expressed in many ways.

   1. What's wrong with marijuana when society legalizes alcohol?

   2. Why not drop acid (LSD) if you gain pleasure, or even spiritual insight, from it?

   3. Since the only thing wrong with marijuana is its illegality, why not use it?

B. For the answers to these questions we must turn to the Bible, God's Word to us. II Timothy 3:16,17. We cannot rely on our reason or cultural attitudes or even our experience to answer this or any other question relating to our moral life with Christ. God must give us the answer.

II. ILLEGAL DRUGS AND WORLDLY VALUES

A. Before accepting Christ we absorbed the values of the world. Ephesians 2:2. But the whole world is under the domination of the devil, our very real adversary, and he offers the world to us in return for our worship of him. I John 5:19; Matthew 4:8,9; Ephesians 6:11,12. For this reason, when we come to Jesus Christ, He calls us to put down the world in all its forms, systems, values, goals, and assumptions. We cannot serve two masters but must deny ourselves, take up our crosses, and follow Him. Matthew 6:24; Mark 8:34.

B. We are thus to present our *bodies* as living and holy sacrifices to God. Romans 12:1. We cannot do this if our bodies continually have fresh needle marks or are spaced out on drugs. Moreover, our bodies are temples of the Holy Spirit, having been bought with a price (the precious blood of Jesus Christ), so that we are to glorify God in our bodies. I Corinthians 6:19,20.

C. We are not to be conformed to this world (or the hip dropout part thereof) but are to be transformed by the renewing of our minds that we might discover and carry out the good, acceptable, and perfect will of God for our lives. Romans 12:2. Our minds are renewed by the Spirit of God—not by drug trips. Drugs come only from the spirit of the world. I Corinthians 2:12.

III. THE FLESH VERSUS THE SPIRIT

A. After receiving Christ we must live with and for Him. This entails fighting the battle between the flesh and the Spirit. By the "flesh" the Bible means not only sexual lust but also any attempt to "do our own thing." God has created us to live in dependence upon Him. Apart from Jesus we can do nothing of eternal merit. John 15:5.

B. Paul's list of the deeds of the flesh includes sorcery and drunkenness. Galatians 5:19-21.

　1. Sorcery is our translation of the Greek word "phar-

makia." From "pharmakia" we get the word "pharmacy." Sorcery is the same as drug use in the Greek because to be a sorcerer is to place people under the control of outside forces, and that is precisely what drugs also do.

2. Alcohol also places an alien force or substance between ourselves and God and hence is part of the devil's system. As a result, drunkenness is also condemned as part of the flesh, and our lives are to be under only the control of the Holy Spirit. Ephesians 5:18.

C. The devil lost us to God for *eternity* when we accepted Jesus Christ as our Lord and Savior, but he has not lost us for *time*. He is busily trying to destroy our potential effectiveness as children of God and thereby defeat the work of God. We must be of sober spirit and on the alert for his tricks. I Peter 5:8. If we are loaded on acid, the devil will make easy prey of us.

D. By the power of the Holy Spirit, we can and must put to death the deeds of the flesh in order to live. Romans 8:12. The result of this yielding of self to the Holy Spirit is the blossoming of the fruit of the Holy Spirit in our lives. Galatians 5:22,23. No drug *ever* produced that quality of love, joy, peace, patience, etc.

IV. THE BODY OF CHRIST AND THE WORLD

A. When Jesus Christ calls us to Himself, He calls us to each other simultaneously. The Christian life is a personal relationship with Christ, but it is not meant to be lived alone. All believers are united by His Spirit to each other and make up His body on earth. I Corinthians 12.

B. Consequently, we have a responsibility not only to the Lord and to ourselves, but also to our brothers and sisters in Christ. Our behavior influences other Christians, and our use of drugs hurts not only ourselves but also the entire Christian family. Paul abstained from eating meat and drinking wine when he thought it might cause a brother to stumble. Romans 14:21; I Corinthians 8:13. How much more this is true of drugs.

C. We must also consider our witness to the world. We are to be lights in the world, holding fast the word of life and abstaining from every form of evil. Philippians 2:15, 16; I Thessalonians 5:22; Ephesians 5:3, 11-12.

V. OBEDIENCE TO THE GOVERNMENT

A. The authority of the state is established by God. Romans 13:1. The Christian is consequently required to submit for the Lord's sake to the state and its laws, *unless* the state interferes with our obedience to Christ. I Peter 2:13; Acts 5:29. See also the outline "The Christian and the State."

B. Inasmuch as the state's attempts to control drug abuse are clearly within the teaching of God's Word, we must obey the law, for this is the will of God.

C. It is important to note that much of the paranoid behavior that is associated with drugs is due to their illegality. A thrill comes from breaking the law and "getting away with it." However, this ego-trip must go when Christ comes.

VI. DRUGS AND THE UNDERWORLD

A. Purchasing illegal drugs is putting money in the hands of the devil, for behind the street hustler stands the underworld, a multi-billion dollar racket. The Mafia ruthlessly destroys people while it builds its own evil empire.

B. All of our money, and for that matter, all of our possessions, belong to God when we accept Jesus Christ. We are to lay up for ourselves treasures in heaven by investing our money, our talents, our time, and ourselves in His work. Matthew 6:20; Romans 12:1.

VII. MISTAKES TO AVOID

A. Don't fall into the trap of thinking that the Christian life is putting down drugs by your own self-effort. Rather, it is the genuine acceptance of Jesus as the Son of God, the Savior and Lord of our lives. God the Holy Spirit enters us and begins to change motives and desires into ones He wants us to have so that we can put down drugs by *His* power.

B. Don't expect to put down drugs and never have to face that temptation again. The devil picks at our weakest points, but that is precisely where the Holy Spirit starts His renovations from within, so when you get the urge to get loaded, claim His power in resisting that temptation. Being tempted is not a sin, but giving in to temptation is. Hebrews 4:15.

C. Don't continue to harbor feelings of guilt on account of any past experiences with drugs. *Whatever* sin you may have committed in the past, Jesus Christ stands before you now and says to you, as He said to the woman caught in the act of adultery (John 8:1-11), *"I do not condemn you. Go your way; from now on sin no more"* Verse 11. No sin is so awful that Christ's shed blood can't cover it. Confess to Him all sins in your past of which you are aware, and believe God's Word that He has *already* forgiven you for them *all.* I John 1:9; Romans 8:1. If Christ has so freely forgiven us, then by what authority can we refuse to forgive ourselves? Through failure and the resulting confession and forgiveness can come growth. We can praise God that someday, when we go to be with Christ or when He comes back to earth in glory, we shall be like Him. Romans 8:29; Philippians 1:6; I John 3:2.

D. Finally, don't isolate yourself from other Christians. This process of becoming like Jesus is not something done alone. Lonely, isolated Christians are defeated Christians. We need each other, and God gives us to each other. Be honest with other brothers and sisters about your needs and hang-ups. Form a fellowship of prayer and sharing together. Learn to love each other in open relationships, pray for each other, rely on each other, and when tempted turn to each other. Jesus says that the mark of our discipleship is our love for one another. John 13:35. What better way is there to love one another than, together, to put down sin and put on Christ?

16

WHAT ABOUT SEX BEFORE MARRIAGE?

Chapter 16
WHAT ABOUT SEX BEFORE MARRIAGE?

I. INTRODUCTION

The "New Morality" of the '60's is already Old Hat. Sexual behavior that used to shock us hardly evokes a raised eyebrow now. Sexual intercourse between a man and woman not married to each other, whether they are middle-aged or sophomores in college, will soon be the rule, not the exception. So the question arises: What about having sexual intercourse with a person to whom you are not married? As Christians dedicated to the discovery and implementation of God's will for our lives, our answer to this question, as to any other, must come not from the ever-changing mores of society but from a careful search of God's unchanging, timeless Word.

II. GOD'S WORD: WAIT UNTIL MARRIAGE

A. Both adultery (sexual intercourse between a married man and a woman not his wife, or between a married woman and a man not her husband) and fornication (sexual intercourse between *any* two people not married to each other) are condemned in Scripture.

1. Adultery is prohibited expressly in the Ten Commandments (Exodus 20:14) and is condemned in many other passages in the Old Testament. Genesis 20:3; Proverbs 6:32-33; Jeremiah 5:7-8.
2. Jesus repeated the commandment prohibiting adultery (Mark 10:19) and even added that looking upon a woman to lust after her amounts to the commission of adultery with her in one's heart. Matthew 5:27-28. Both adultery and fornication are condemned by Him in Mark 7:20-23. See also Mark 10:11-12.
3. One of the few "essentials" that the apostles felt necessary to touch upon in their letter to the Antioch Christians was that they abstain from fornication. Acts 15:28-29.
4. Paul speaks out strongly against sex outside of marriage in many of his letters. For example:
   a. I Corinthians 6:9-20—Paul warns us that those who continue to practice fornication or adultery "shall not inherit the kingdom of God." Verses 9-10. He adds that "our bodies are not for sexual immorality, but for the Lord." verse 13. Indeed, our bodies are "members of Christ" (verse 15) and "temples of the Holy Spirit" who is in us (verse 19). Accordingly, we are to glorify God in our bodies (verse 20) by fleeing sexual immorality (verse 18).
   b. Galatians 5:19-23—Sexual immorality, impurity, sensuality, and carousings are all included in Paul's list of the "deeds of the flesh," the doers of which "shall not inherit the kingdom of God." We are to display the fruit of the Holy Spirit, which includes love, patience, faithfulness, and self-control.
   c. Ephesians 5:3-12—Paul urges the Ephesian Christians not to let sexual immorality or impurity "even be named" among them. Verse 3. Moreover, not only are they not to participate in the "unfruitful deeds of darkness," but they are even to expose them. Verse 11.
   d. See also Romans 13:9; I Corinthians 5:9-11; 10:8; II

Corinthians 12:21; Colossians 3:5-7; I Thessalonians 4:1-8; II Timothy 2:22.

5. Other New Testament authors were equally emphatic in their condemnation of sex outside of marriage. Hebrews 13:4; James 2:11; II Peter 2:9-16; Jude 7; Revelation 2:20-22; 9:21.

B. An example of a Biblical figure who "fled" from sexual immorality is Joseph. Genesis 39:7-12. His master's wife asked him repeatedly, day after day, to lie with her, but Joseph refused each time: "How then could I do this great evil, and sin *against God?*" Verse 9. One day when he was doing his work around the house, she caught him by his garment and asked him again. Understanding the seriousness of this temptation, Joseph "left his garment in her hand and fled, and went outside." Verse 12.

III. WHY GOD SAYS TO WAIT

Given that God says to wait for sexual fulfillment until marriage, the question remains: *Why* does He make this demand of us? To answer this question, we must first look at Scripture to see what His purposes are in creating us as sexual beings.

A. Creation of man and woman—Genesis 2

1. After creating the man, God made this remarkable statement: "It is not good for man to be alone." Verse 18. Adam's relationship with God, important as that is, is not enough for Adam. There are certain needs that God has built into us that can only be fulfilled in relationship with another human being.

2. So God made a "helper suitable for him." Verse 18. Thus, man and woman were created for companionship, to enjoy life together. In passing, we note that to meet Adam's needs God created a woman, not six women (polygamy) or another man (homosexuality).

3. The interpretation of this event is given in verse 24: "For this cause a man shall *leave* his father and his mother, and

shall *cleave* to his wife; and they shall become one flesh." Becoming "one flesh" refers not only to sexual union but to the *totality* of their union. The context of this total union is thus a radical break with the past (the "leaving") and a total commitment for the present and future (the "cleaving").

4. The result is given in verse 25: "And the man and his wife were both naked and were *not ashamed.*" There is no shame in sexual union. In the right context, sexual union is not dirty but very beautiful, exciting, and holy.

B. Fall of man—Genesis 3

1. Succumbing to the serpent's temptations, Adam and Eve ate the forbidden fruit. Verse 6. The result of their sin is that they were separated from God and from each other: now man and woman are naked and *ashamed,* and they make loin coverings for themselves out of fig leaves. Verse 7. Their freedom, joy, and fulfillment are broken. The serpent had told them they would be "like God, knowing good and evil" (verse 5), but they got only the knowledge that they were naked.

2. Thus, sin distracts us from our commitments—to God and to each other. Since we can know ourselves only when we are in commitment to Him, sin plunges us into an identity crisis. We are like scraps of paper in the air, wafting aimlessly to and fro. As sin does its dirty work in every area of our lives, it should come as no surprise to us that we all have problems with our sexuality.

C. Redemption of man through Jesus Christ

1. God sent His Son Jesus Christ not only to redeem us from the *penalty* of sin (eternal punishment), but also to free us from the *power* of sin over us. Christ came to undo what sin has done to us, to put us back together, to give us our identity, to make us whole persons in commitment to Him. Unlike forgiveness, which we receive immediately and completely, this wholeness does not come overnight. We are "goods in process."

2. In the context of our sexual lives, Jesus wants, first of all, to remove our "blinders" (sin) and open our eyes to see God's purposes in creating us as sexual beings. He wants to change our selfish preoccupation with the *what* in sex to an understanding of the *why*.

D. God's purposes in creating us as sexual beings

  1. We have already seen from Genesis 2 that God created man and woman for companionship. He made us male and female, *equal but not equivalent,* so that we might complement each other.

  2. In addition, and it hardly needs to be stated, God has chosen to use sexual union between man and woman as His way of bringing new lives into our world.

  3. But what is perhaps God's greatest purpose in creating us as sexual beings is one seen most clearly in Ephesians 5:21-33, where Paul analogizes marriage to the relationship between Jesus Christ and the Church, the body of all believers in Him.

    a. In the context of our subjecting ourselves to one another in the body of Christ (verse 21), the wife is to place herself, *voluntarily,* in subjection to her husband in the same way that she does to the Lord. Verse 22. That's a pretty strong statement, and there are those who would take this verse out of its context and classify Paul as a "male chauvinist pig." However, note that Paul goes on to address the husband, too, and he makes what is perhaps an even greater demand of him: "Husbands, love your wives, just as Christ also loved the church and *gave Himself up for her. . . .*" Verse 25. Wives, you are to be subject in marriage to a husband who loves you in the same way that Jesus does. That's not manipulation but self-giving, self-sacrificing love. If a woman can't subject herself to that kind of nourishing, protecting, and cherishing, then she can't subject herself to Christ either. Thus, God's purpose is that *in total union with a person of the* *opposite sex, we might manifest the same love that Jesus has for us.* Christian marriages can provide a very effective witness of God's unconditional love for man.

b. This purpose helps to explain why God tells us to wait for sexual union until marriage. Just as Christ gave up His life for us, so a Christian man and woman who want to be united sexually must each sacrifice for the sake of the other by making a radical break with their past (the "leaving" of Genesis 2:24). And just as Jesus has committed Himself to us for all eternity, promising never to desert nor forsake us (Hebrews 13:5; Matthew 28:20), so a man and woman in Christ who want sexual union must commit themselves to each other " 'til death do they part" (the "cleaving"). This commitment, like our commitment to Christ, is to be made publicly, with the community of believers standing with the man and woman as they commit their lives to God and to each other. Needless to say, this sacrifice and commitment is not to be lightly entered into. But to opt for sexual union without both this sacrifice and this public commitment is to fail to understand—or worse yet, to care—that God has ordained that sexual union be nothing less than a human illustration of His self-sacrificing, unconditional love for us. Thus, the Christian in God's will waits for sex until marriage not because of a low view of sex, but—on the contrary—because he holds such a high view of sex that he cannot allow it to be reduced to a means of pleasure only.

E. Excursus: Two divine callings—marriage and celibacy
From the above one might be tempted to conclude that God's perfect will for *all* of us includes marriage and sexual union within that marriage. In fact, society tends to place a certain stigma upon those who haven't married by an age which it deems to be appropriate. But, as is often the case, God's Word has something very different to tell us.

191

1. Marriage is seen by our Lord Jesus Christ as an act of God: "What therefore *God* has joined together, let no man separate." Mark 10:9. And, as we have seen, Paul exhibited a very high view of marriage in Ephesians 5:21-33. See also I Timothy 4:1-3.

2. However, marriage is not to be the Christian's primary concern in life. Jesus reminds us that our first love is always to be *Him:* if anyone "does not hate his own father and mother and wife and children and brothers and sisters, yes, and even his own life" in comparison with his love for Him, he will not be able to be His disciple. Luke 14:26. Jesus also taught that in the resurrection there will be no marriages. Mark 12:25. Thus, to decide upon a life partner is to make the *second* most important decision of one's life.

3. Moreover, Christ taught that *both* marriage and celibacy are divine callings. Matthew 19:11-12. Marriage is only "for those to whom it has been given." Verse 11. One who is able to accept life without a spouse, for the sake of the kingdom of heaven, is urged by Christ to accept it. Verse 12. Indeed, Christ Himself never married. Paul, also unmarried, elaborates upon this in I Corinthians 7, where he points out the major advantage of single life—a greater opportunity for undistracted devotion and service to the Lord. Verses 32-35. While urging those who are single to remain single (e.g. verses 7, 8, 26, 40), Paul emphasizes that this is his opinion and not the Lord's command (e.g. verses 8, 25-26, 35, 40). More importantly, he repeats Christ's teaching that both marriage and celibacy are gifts from God. Verses 7, 17.

4. Accordingly, marriage in God's view is not a matter of course. Marriage seems to be His will for most of us, but for many reasons some Christians will never get married. Marriage may be expedient or inexpedient for us, depending upon our particular personalities, gifts, and talents and the purposes—short-term and long-term

which God has for our lives. The challenge of single life which Paul offers in I Corinthians 7 is one which all Christians, single and married, should respect. Certainly, we have no right to look with disfavor upon the calling of another.

IV. COMMON OBJECTIONS TO WAITING UNTIL MARRIAGE

A. *Objection*: Sex is a natural drive given to me by God. When I'm hungry, I eat. When I'm "sexy," I have sex. How can something which is so much fun be wrong?

Answer:

1. The analogy between food and sex is extremely weak: Do you view your partner in sex like a bowl of corn flakes or a T-bone steak? Our pleasure-satiated culture drums it into us that men and women are mere objects to be used rather than people to relate to, but that's an abomination to our Father and Creator.

2. It is agreed that our sexual drives are God-given, but the issue is what the appropriate context for the fulfillment of those drives is. Jesus Christ wants to share your sex life by being the mediator between you and your husband or wife. He wants to unite you spiritually as well as physically and emotionally, in the context of your total commitment to Him and to each other. Without Him as mediator in your marriage, you can never have a satisfactory sexual relationship. It is interesting that many guys want to experiment before marriage and yet also want to marry virgins.

B. *Objection*: What's wrong with having sex so long as it doesn't hurt anybody, e.g. if we both consent, are in love, and have committed ourselves to each other, but we can't get married right away for financial reasons? Besides, thanks to the pill, there is no fear of children.

Answer:

1. Even with the pill, mistakes do occur. Do you want to

assume even a 1% risk of having to build your entire life on an accidental pregnancy?

2. Moreover, that possibility aside, how do you *know* that you aren't going to hurt each other? Are you omniscient? What do you know about his or her conscience, about his or her sensitivity to the Holy Spirit, about his or her desire to live according to God's Word? How do you know you won't leave deep spiritual and psychological scars in your sexual partner? You don't.

3. Finally, how do you know that you aren't going to hurt yourself? You don't—you have no way of knowing. The assumption that you won't is merely a rationalization. Since you are violating God's Word, you *are* hurting yourself and your boy or girl friend. In particular, once you have yielded to temptation you are likely to find it extremely difficult to keep from doing so again with any guy or girl you are with and are attracted to. Sex is such a deep, intimate sharing of the totality of your lives that when it's right, it's very right, and when it's wrong, it's very wrong.

C. *Objection*: No one buys a pair of shoes until he's tried them on. In the same way, isn't sexual intercourse necessary preparation for a happy marriage? Moreover, isn't intercourse necessary so that I can find out whether my partner is capable of bearing a child?

Answer: No.

1. Now one's sexual partner is being compared to a pair of shoes. Note how depersonalizing all of the commonly heard analogies for sex are.

2. The assumption that a man and a woman can establish sexual compatibility before marriage is a myth. In marriage, the sex act takes place under completely different conditions: there is no rush, no fear of being discovered, no fear of being betrayed by the other, and no fear of pregnancy. In light of this, how can we test sexual compatibility in a motel or in the back seat of a

ar? Chances are that the woman will be somewhat frigid and afraid, or that the man will find himself impotent out of fear and guilt. Are you going to write one another off for that? To do so would be absurd. There are complex psychological factors involved in sex, in addition to the physical factors. God's will is that we trust in Him to show us His life partner for us and then, with His guidance, get used to each other gradually and correct together any awkwardness and minor difficulties that may exist in our sexual relationship as the marriage begins.

3. As for the fear of marrying a person who is unable to bear a child, again the exhortation to trust God's leading in choosing your life partner, rather than your own experimentation, applies. Moreover, as we have seen, the Bible clearly teaches that child-bearing is not the sole, or even the main, purpose of marriage. Complete fulfillment occurs in the union of husband and wife, spiritually and emotionally as well as sexually, when the two become "one flesh." Genesis 2:24. It can also be added that one of the causes of barrenness in a woman is, ironically, the *fear* of barrenness and the related fear that her husband might leave her if she doesn't bear a child. A woman needs affirmation from her man that he loves her as she is, whether she is ever able to bear him a child or not.

4. Excursus: For those who are compatibility test-minded, here are five areas of our lives in which we can test the strength of our relationship with a person of the opposite sex:

    a. Spiritual—Is he (she) a Christian? Paul is clear in his teaching that if we do choose to marry, it must be "in the Lord." I Corinthians 7:39. Moreover, are the two of you at comparable stages of spiritual maturity, or is one always ministering to the other? Do you pray and read God's Word together?

    b. Social—Do you have friends you like to [...] together? Or do the two of you have two very [...] types of people as your friends?

    c. Recreational—Do you have fun together? Do yo[...] share some of the same interests— reading, listening to music, going to the beach, hiking, playing tennis?

    d. Intellectual—Do you carry on serious conversations with each other? Do you stimulate each other's minds?

    e. Physical—Are you attracted to each other? To put it bluntly, do you want him (her) for your bed-mate for life? Probably most of us tend to place too much emphasis on this one, at the expense of other more objective criteria.

    Where there is compatibility and growth in all five of these areas, sex can—in marriage—become the fulfillment of that total union.

D. *Objection*: I need to have sex with my boy or girl friend to find out whether he or she really loves me. For if he or she loves me, he or she will meet my needs, and I need sex.

    Answer: What kind of love demands this kind of proof? Selfish love. Can you build a marriage on that? It has been well said that lust cannot wait to have, but love can wait to give. In fact, getting your boy or girl friend into bed with you doesn't prove his or her love for you at all, but merely proves that both of you are in bondage to your sexual drives or perhaps to the attitudes of your peers. Having sex to prove the genuineness of your love is merely a cop-out for relating personally over a period of time. There are far better ways of discovering whether or not he or she really loves you. For example, how accepting of your faults is he or she? How does he or she react to cancelled plans due to your getting sick?

E. *Objection*: I need to have sex to show that I am a man (or woman).

    Answer: What made Jesus Christ a man was His perfect obedience to His Father. In the same way it is our

ience to God, not our sex life, which makes us men and
en. Contrary to what our culture may tell us, Jesus
ist, not the experience of having sex, gives us our
nhood (or womanhood) and straightens out our identity
sis as we trust in Him moment by moment.

BENEFITS OF WAITING UNTIL MARRIAGE

A. No guilt—God tells us to wait until marriage. Not waiting
will create guilt that will hamper our relationships with
Him, with your sexual partner, and with everyone else. By
waiting you can know, because God says so, that Jesus
Christ smiles on your marriage bed.

B. No fear—Waiting ensures that you will never have to be
afraid, not even to the extent of one fleeting thought, to
having to build a marriage on an unexpected pregnancy.

C. No comparison—Waiting ensures that you will never fall
into the devastating trap of comparing your spouse's sexual
performance with that of a previous sexual partner.

D. Spiritual growth—On the positive side, waiting will help you
subject your physical drives to the Lordship of Christ, and
thereby develop your self-control, an important aspect of
the fruit of the Holy Spirit. Also, if you get married and are
later separated temporarily (e.g. for a business trip), then
this discipline early in your relationship will give both of
you confidence and trust in each other during that time of
separation.

E. Greater joy—Waiting ensures that there will be something
saved for your marriage relationship, for that first night and
for the many nights thereafter. The anticipation of the
fulfillment of your relationship in sexual union is exciting.
Don't spoil it by jumping the gun.

VI. HOW FAR SHALL WE GO BEFORE MARRIAGE?

Given our conviction to refrain from sexual intercourse
until marriage, the question remains: How far shall we go,

short of sexual intercourse, before marriage?

A. The answer to this question depends both upon ║
along you are in your relationship (e.g. first d║
engaged) and upon your abilities to withstand th║
strong temptation to have sexual intercourse.

B. However, a general principle which we feel applies║
everyone is the following: *That which has its natural end* ║
sexual intercourse should be held to your wedding night.

  1. This means, at the very least, that heavy petting, i.e. direct
stimulation of each other's sexual organs, and mutual
masturbation should be out. Don't build up your sexual
drives and desires to the point of no return, lest your
physical relationship become a source of frustration
rather than of joy for you.

  2. This also means that you should not engage in any
physical activity which will build up the *other* person's
sexual drives to the point of no return. In the context of a
different problem, that of eating certain types of food,
Paul puts forth the general exhortation that we not do
anything which causes our brother (or sister) to stumble.
Romans 14:13, 21. Thus, both persons must be sensitive
to each other and must place the other's spiritual health
ahead of their own desire for physical fulfillment now.
When in doubt, don't! For "whatever is not from faith is
sin." Romans 14:23. Pray, alone and together, about your
physical relationship—if you can't visualize Jesus Christ
smiling at the two of you, the Holy Spirit may be urging
you to pull back the reins a little, for the sake of your love
for the Lord and for him (her).

C. This does not mean that the two of you are not going to
relate physically before marriage, nor does it mean that
your sexual drives won't increase as you do relate physically. And it certainly doesn't mean that you won't want to
go to bed with each other. But it does mean that the two of
you will make Jesus Christ the Lord of your sexual life, and
that you are going to wait for the green light from Him.

the risen Jesus Christ at the center of your lives,
ment by moment, and ask Him to give you the strength
need to wait.

lk together honestly about your physical relationship,
nd in particular, about the pre-marital limits to your
physical relationship. Moreover, help each other by what
you wear, where you go, and what you do, especially in the
later hours of the evening.

C. Enlist the aid of the Christian community. Paul urges us to
bear each other's burdens; James, to confess our sins to one
another. Galatians 6:2; James 5:16. Find a small body of
Christians or several trusted friends of the same sex and
share your struggle with them. Don't go it alone!

VIII. "I DO NOT CONDEMN YOU"

A. Feelings of guilt arising from a sex-related sin are particularly difficult to shake. However, know this: *Whatever*
sexual sin you may have committed in the past, Jesus Christ
stands before you now and says to you, as He said to the
woman caught in the act of adultery (John 8:1-11), "Neither
do I condemn you; go your way; from now on sin no
more." Verse 11.

B. *No sin* is so awful that Christ's shed blood can't cover it.
"There is therefore *now no condemnation* for those who are
in Christ Jesus." Romans 8:1. "If we confess our sins, [God]
is faithful and righteous to forgive us our sins and to cleanse
us from all unrighteousness." I John 1:9. If Christ has so
freely forgiven us, then we can, and must, forgive ourselves
and forge ahead, prepared and preprayered to send Jesus to
the door the next time Satan knocks!

IX. CONCLUSION

God's word to us concerning sex is not no, but *yes—yes in
marriage*, where there is companionship; where we're
helpmates, fit for each other; where there is sacrifice,

including a radical break with the past; where ther[...]
long commitment to live with and cherish one [...]
where this commitment has been made before t[...]
powers that be and before the body of Christ; and[...]
there is a union of the totality of our lives. In Christ, s[...]
very beautiful thing.

CONCLUSION

If you have received Jesus Christ as your Savior and Lord, then you have been called to be faithful in seeking to discover and carry out God's will for your life. We have suggested that His will for you is twofold:

(1) That you grow up into maturity in Christ (Part I), as evidenced, for example, by a greater understanding of God's Word and its applications in your own life, a greater faithfulness in prayer, and a greater desire to exercise your spiritual gifts to the purpose of building up the body of believers; and

(2) That you move out into the world (Part II), proclaiming—by word and by deed—the availability of the abundant life offered by Christ, and at the same time resisting the temptation to be conformed to the evil in the world. In the hope of assisting you in your striving to be faithful to both of these aspects of God's will for your life, we have presented dozens, if not hundreds, of scriptural commands

and some of our own practical suggestions concern[...]
to carry out those commands.

An important and comforting teaching of Scrip[...] deserves to be repeated! With every command God [...] His people the promise that He will not leave them fl[...] in their own futile efforts to carry out the command. W[...] permission He will work in them to accomplish that wi[...] has called them to do. For example, Paul wrote to [...] Philippians: "Keep on working out your salvation . . . *for* it [...] God who is at work in you, both to will and to work for His good pleasure." Philippians 2:12-13. The doctrine of divine enablement is not only consistent with the doctrine of Christian responsibility, but also indispensable to it. You *can* carry out the commands of Scripture because, and only because, Jesus Christ has entered your life and is working in you to make you the person He wants you to become.

The author of the epistle to the Hebrews captured this truth in his benediction, which we offer as our prayer for you: "Now may the God of peace . . . equip you in every good thing to do His will, working in you that which is pleasing in His sight, through Jesus Christ, to whom be the glory forever and ever. Amen." Hebrews 13:20-21.

notes